THE PASSENGERS

THE

PASSENGERS

WILL

ASHON

faber

First published in 2022
by Faber & Faber Ltd
Bloomsbury House
74–77 Great Russell Street
London WCIB 3DA

Typeset by Faber & Faber Ltd
Printed and bound by CPI Group (UK) Ltd, Croydon, CR0 4YY

A CIP record for this book
is available from the British Library

ISBN 978–0–571–36414–5

2 4 6 8 10 9 7 5 3 1

Each of the following sections represents a different voice.

'Chance has always been my best assistant.'
AGNÈS VARDA

1.

I want to stay and stay and never go.

2.

So that's the thing. Like you said, it's interconnected. Every-thing is interconnected.

3.

Life is a flux. It's constantly moving. It's like a river—it just carries on, it happens and moves, it changes.

4.

It's beautiful to share, you know. I think we are here to share. Share happiness, share love, share our things. Our things are not for ourselves. They are better when we share them.

5.

We stopped next to these fir trees and my daughter said,
What's that noise? What's going on? We're looking around
for this strange buzzing sound, for this noise. And eventually
we looked up and the trees were covered, literally covered,
in bees.

6.

There's so much room for projection. You can read anything into anything. Sometimes when I'm sad I'll text my boyfriend and then, whatever he replies it will read as unsympathetic. You know what I mean? It doesn't really matter what it says because you're in that headspace.

7.

I see a bit of mopping up ahead. I do think it's had an effect on some people's mindset, in terms of going out, doing normal things. It's really affected people's mental health, a lot of people. What's next is very much, I don't know how to put it, but almost realigning ourselves back to day-to-day living.

8.

I tried killing myself. I tried hanging myself after I come
out. It actually helped with my PTSD because I've got brain
damage to me memory, so I can't remember a lot of me time
in the army, do you know what I mean? It kinda worked,
kinda helped in a way, yeah [laughs]. I was hanging for that
long that I damaged me memory.

9.

I'm moving waste, so regardless of recession or them putting the walls up or closing borders or making it difficult for trade and all the rest of it, it doesn't really affect me that much. Because London produces waste and it's always going to. Do you know what I mean? It's got to go. It doesn't matter what state of the economy or what affairs are going on, waste has got to move.

10.

It's almost like a puzzle. You have to construct in your head what's going on. Which can be different things, depending on what you see. You don't know what's going on and it's like this is a message for you. This is the note that tells you what's going on and you need to understand it but then you can't really read it. It's like a message in a bottle. It doesn't say something about a particular time in history but it's like a construction of that period instead.

11.

I believe that there are people in life who you meet for a
certain reason—and people can bring out certain aspects
of your character that maybe you didn't know were there.
You've met them for a reason and they're beneficial to
whoever you become or whoever you're destined to become.
At school we moved classes, so I got split up from my friends,
but actually it turned out to be one of the best things that
could've happened. I met so many new people who I feel
really changed my life. People come into your life for a
reason, because of fate.

12.

I've been living here for a couple years but I've visited many times. Before I was born my parents lived here in the community. My parents actually met in the community and moved away when my mum was pregnant. They visited multiple times with me when I was growing up, for a week here and there. Some of my earliest memories are just randomly playing around the island. All the gardens have granite walls around them, and almost every young, active child who comes here wants to patrol the walls and walk around all the tops of the walls, around all the gardens, around all the houses. I remember doing that a lot when I was young.

13.

There's not a lot of stuff that you can do about it to be fair. You've gotta try and rationalise it yourself. Speaking to people about it really helps—getting your feelings out and talking to others. I try and play a lot of sports. I play a lot of tennis and things like that just to try and calm me mind and whatnot. But yeah, it's just really, really difficult. You've got to really try and keep yourself busy. And in my job it's difficult, to be fair, because I spend so much time driving. Things just pop into my head for no particular reason whatsoever and then you're sitting on your own re-thinking about it, re-thinking about it. And the craziest thing about it is you're always questioning everything you do.

14.

His mum dreamed it was the Resurrection Day. The end of
the world. She was out on a beach with the whole family
and all of a sudden the waves of the sea were going all on
top of us. And the whole world, every single person in the
world, just came to where that sea is. And the water was
going on top of us. I was running, trying to get to shelter or
whatever. But there was nowhere to go—except that sea. In
this particular dream, while everybody is running into that
sea and getting under that particular wave that's coming
through, she was saying, *Repent to God, repent to God,
repent to God.* Cos what's about to happen is worse. In our
religion we do translate dreams. It's like a shaken message,
y'know? It just shakes you, type of thing.

15.

It looks like it's wobbly. The ground looks like it's shaking or something. Because the pieces don't quite fit, so it looks like it's wobbly. The person might be wobbling. It looks like an optical illusion, because she's standing but it looks like she's sitting down at the same time. I think he took a picture and then maybe split the picture into pieces, like maybe gradually cut it and then fixed it together. It looks like it is one thing but then you realise it's lots of little pieces. Like, this would be one country, that would be another country, that would be a different country. It would look like it's one picture, but it would be lots of different pictures. Then you can kind of tell a story, cos there'll be lots of ideas. Otherwise if you actually know what's happening, it's not that interesting.

16.

I have a pathological aversion to hairdressers. I think I've
had my hair cut professionally once in about thirty years.
The first thing I'd do on leaving the hairdresser's, which
was terrible—I'd rub my head on the doormat as vigorously
as I could. Part of the reasoning was so that I wouldn't be
taken back because it would be too embarrassing. Related to
all of this, I have probably only washed my hair under ten
times since I was eighteen, which I attribute to not going
bald. Actually, I think there might be something in that. I
don't know, it's been suggested by other people. I am such an
anomaly in the breadth of my family, it could be one of the
reasons in terms of hair growth. If a bird shat in my hair, I'd
probably wash it. Actually I wouldn't, you wouldn't need to,
I'd just rinse it out.

17.

It was a Tommasini, an Italian frame, but it'd been painted up in this Midlands bike shop. It's hard to describe. The paintwork was shiny, that kind of oil-on-water effect, so it's cream but with a kind of oily water finish. And it had really straight tubes, lovely, really thin. I think it's really aesthetically pleasing. It's like the drawing that a child does of a bicycle. What I got really into as well were the lug works. That's where bits of the tubing join together. Back in the day they would have these little separate pieces, lugs, and they started becoming really decorative. Tommasini has a little *T* cut out in the bottom bracket. It's the care. You look at it, and you look at all the different things that have gone into it, and it's something that someone made with their hands, and did it with a lot of skill. It's an object made with love.

18.

I'm a bit of a thingy me, I like a bit of speed. If I was in the car we'd have you home by now. It were only a Seat Leon. Did 170 mile an hour didn't it? 170 mile an hour. Three and a half hundred brake, only weighed 1.3 ton. Sounded like the old T5, you know the old police T5s? It sounded like that. Only a little two-litre turbo. It were alright. Had a couple of police chases in that one. It were quick enough. It must have been quick enough because they didn't knock on my door. So yeah, it were quick enough. You know the big AMGs on the motorway? Don't get me wrong, from a start it'd have me, but they're restricted to 155, them. So on the motorway, we're racing with them, obviously we're both sailing, soon as they hit 155 I'm carrying on in my little Leon: *See you in a bit!*

19.

I was on a road with double cars parked both sides, single-lane traffic. It was raining and I don't know why, there was no way she could overtake me, there was no room, but she tried to and I think it was her wing mirror clipped my handlebars. Pretty sure it was my handlebars. It all happened very quickly, but I felt the impact and the bike went from under me. Fortunately, I got a foot on the ground and then I sort of fell on my bike. But I got to my feet really fast because, you know, I was in the road. And she looked back and saw me get to my feet and just went. Left me there. So I walked home. I was pretty rattled. And because it was pouring with rain there weren't many people out and about so there was no one to say, *Are you alright?* or whatever. The rest of the traffic went on and that was it. I just walked home and it was horrible.

20.

My boyfriend broke up with me fifteen days ago. It was my fault and I still love him desperately. One week later I had to drive into London to get the last of my things before lockdown, and go to my orthodontist to have my braces tightened. I'm twenty-seven and I have braces. Don't even talk to me about it. His house is only five minutes out of my way if I'm driving down the A3 to go home from mine to my parents'. Without even thinking about it, I turned left at the petrol station, not even quite sure of the directions, never having driven it myself. But I didn't make one wrong turn. And five minutes later I was driving down his street. I drove slowly. There was no one behind me. His mother has put up a picture of a rainbow drawn by a child facing up out of their living room window. His car wasn't there. I knew it wouldn't be. He's in Cornwall with friends. It was only ten minutes of my life, but I haven't told anyone about that detour.

21.

Doing nothing is not good for you. It's a cycle of depression.
When I start therapy, the therapist explained to me—do
something with people [to] change your mood. Just to break
the lock. When you are completely down, you don't want [to]
leave your bed, your room, but you have to push yourself.
Last year, I know two or three people died in this system. Two
woman and one man. Just in this year. They died. They died
and it was a shock for all of us. It's not a game. It's serious on
people—a lost life. And this is a process. Sometime you start
well and the system break you. The system work like that.
It's a kind of moral pressure. They just do it. They can send
to you a letter saying, *Come with all your stuff. Come with
your suitcase.* It's intimidation. And so when you are not
strong, your blood pressure just starts increasing. It's very
stressful, going to sign. You choose to claim asylum, you
need support, you need protection, you need a safe place. But
in practice the system is the opposite.

22.

I like rainbows because of the spectrum. They have a range of everything and they have things that we can't see that are there. It's kind of a simple thing but it can lead to places, like the pot of the gold. The pot of the gold [laughs]. I think it's a journey and it's a path and it's a hope. I was just reading an article about hope. I've always thought hope's quite a negative emotion in a way. It's passive. When we were growing up if we ever said anything was nice, Dad always said, *What do you actually mean? That's such an undescriptive term.* And I think hope can be a bit like that—I hope for something but how does that actually happen, or what does that mean? It's good to be reminded that it can be a much stronger positive. And I think it's what the rainbows represent, in a way. Living how I do, it's a very privileged life. Things which seem hard actually aren't hard, compared to so many people. Our lives are much lighter than people who have bigger, much more real burdens and challenges. And yeah, I think we need to remember to appreciate the lightness.

23.

I got bunged off to boarding school. There were four Irish girls at school, and we were collectively known as the *green wogs*, which was nice, wasn't it? This was an English school in the middle of Wales. The Welsh thought that all the girls at school were English. This one afternoon the Welsh girls were speaking in English, saw us, broke into Welsh, and as soon as we'd crossed them by a certain distance, they turned back and yelled, *English snobs!* And I just found myself yelling, *I'm not an English snob, I'm an Irish snob!*

Northern Ireland has a lot of Gaelic loan-words that are used in everyday speech, so when I came to England, I sounded like everyone else, but vast swathes of what I said were completely incomprehensible. People were looking at me with a furrowed brow and I sort of judged that this must be a word that people don't understand. It was rather sad, actually, that I had to censor my language so that it could be understood. That annoyed me at the time, and when I go back [to Northern Ireland] now it's almost immediate—I land and my vocabulary changes. It's like getting into a nice warm bath. It's delightful to use proper words again.

24.

To be fair, I've had some weird dates. This is really embarrassing—I went to Laser Quest. It was just us two in the whole thing cos no one else was in there. He was really up for it cos he's a bit weird. And he's older as well, which was even weirder. Like, *Why are you, an adult, wanting to do this?* I was just like, *Oh, haha, sounds fun!* But inside: *That's literally not at all what I wanna do.* I could not think of anything worse than to fucking go to Laser Quest.

We met on a train and then, I can't remember who it was, whether he asked for my number or he gave me [his]. I think he got mine. And then, cos he lived in Bristol, he was like, *Do you wanna come to Bristol? You can come to mine, we can go out and have a day of things.* And then I got there and he was like, *Yeah, I decided we can go [to] Laser Quest.* And I was like, *Fuck, I shoulda just not come.* Now with social media as well, you get home, and they're like, *HOW ARE YOU?* And I'm like, *Oh my god.* You can never stop talking anymore. You can never end a conversation.

25.

Stitching together these images fucks with our perspective. Perspective is our reality, so do we actually work with absolutes? We have conventional absolutes, because of the limitations of our physical body—like, *The sky is blue*. The sky is blue because that's how our eyes register the filtering of light through our atmosphere. That's a conventional absolute. But what would it be like for animals with different eyes? They don't see blue, do they? Dogs are supposed to see in black and white. The sky isn't blue to them. And so, for instance, what's rude to one person isn't rude to another. And that's based on perspective. We're always, in every second, creating our own reality, rebuilding it. We just don't know, because the way our brain works, it fills in all the gaps. If we're looking, our brain can fill in the peripheral gaps, even though we might not actually physically be seeing them. Even a table is made up of molecules that are in constant motion but for us they're solid. Everything is finite. We like to think that the universe is infinite, but as long as you can measure it, it's finite, right? Everything's finite, whether it be samples in a song or molecules in a table, or packets of memories stitched together. They're basically like quanta, right? They're stitched together. So it mirrors the fabric of our actual physical reality as part of the universe.

26.

This is a story about fear. I don't suppose it is to my credit, but anyway, here we go.

Once I was staying in a very boring bit of a very boring city, when I thought I'd like to make myself a bit of an adventure. So one night, rather than morning, one night I got up very early to walk, during the night, out to a fishing village near the town, which was actually quite pretty. I wanted to go down on to the waterfront of the village and watch the sun come up.

Up I got, in the middle of the night, and walked fairly fast along the coast road until I came to the village. I looked down the hill towards the waterfront and I could see not a thing. Not a light on in any of the houses, not a light on any of the fishing boats that were still in the harbour, though most were out fishing. It was totally black. With the starlight at my back and darkness in front of me, I couldn't physically make myself walk down the hill towards the village and the adventure I'd set myself, to watch the sun come up. And so, within minutes, I'd turned round in despair, leaving the darkness behind, and through the last of the starlight, the first of the dawn, back I went to my boring digs in my boring little bit of town.

27.

Something that always makes me laugh is that whenever I tell anyone I'm Jewish they go, *Oh yeah, I can tell, you look Jewish.* And I'd say I look the absolute spitting image of [my father], who actually isn't Jewish. But once someone knows who you are, they put that on to how they look at you. I think you stop looking at people after you've met them a few times. As soon as you know roughly what someone looks like, you don't really scrutinise their appearance at all. So the big, memorable things—like people know I've got brown hair, it's a bit curly, what length it is, blue eyes, roughly what kind of height and build I am—that's all you really see when you're looking at someone. Which is why it's funny when someone tells you, *Oh my god, you look exactly like my friend* and they show you a picture and you think, *Oh, that looks nothing like me.* I do think after you've met someone a few times you just have this image of them in your head. You don't properly, properly look at them. Which is why it's always funny when you see someone for the first time after a while and think, *Oh, I don't remember you looking like that.* They just have a vague category for how you look. Yeah, once you have an image of someone in your head it's quite easy to just categorise.

28.

Years ago, my sister knew this guru who was called G____,
from Germany, and he came over to Harrow. Indian guy, he
was part of an ashram in Pondicherry. What was it called? I
can't remember the movement, but she was always talking
about G____ and she was really into this spiritual movement,
and she said, *I'm gonna take you and introduce you to him.*
I thought he was a very comical character. He got hold of my
hand and dragged me through the house and just stood and
looked at me, and I was giggling: *What an odd little man.*
He was looking at me, and then he spoke to my sister in
German, and he said, *She will receive grace.* [My sister] went,
He's never said that to me, and I went, *I have no idea what
he means, so thanks, but I don't know what you're talking
about.* He said, *You're like a little girl,* and I went, *Oh, okay.*
And I kind of just forgot about that.

I never believed in religion but when I found God, when
I actually connected to this profound energy, I completely
understood it, because the way that I would summarise grace
is that there is a sense of being cradled by something that's
so pure and so light and so knowledgeable and so dependable
that the weight of the world falls away, and all that's left
is you and that. That's how I would describe grace. It's a
profound feeling of comfort. And also I think it takes away all
the fears that you've ever had in life.

29.

When I look at a cat, I feel like it could be a god [laughs]. Cats are so perfect, they just seem to have been created with such perfection in their nature, their beauty, the way they're so affectionate but so playful and unpredictable, I feel they're almost divine.

We got our first cat when I was about ten, so my mum converted me to loving cats, really. My current cat—who I'm looking at as I'm speaking to you—is seventeen years old, and she is a really wonderful cat and doing really well for her age as well. Also I don't have children and I don't think I could have children so the cat, I must admit the cat is a bit of a child substitute. I sort of love her like she's my kid.

I don't know if cats are quite as independent as people say. I think there's a slight myth in that. It's true that you can go out for a day. It seems like you can't just go off and leave a dog for too long, and with a cat you can. But I do think if you give them a lot of love, they open up and become more loving, but then they miss you more if you're away and it's harder on them. I was once away for two and a half weeks, and when I came back she was a different sort of cat. She'd kinda withdrawn a bit and she'd gone a bit funny and she was a bit psychologically dead. And then after a day or two she flowered back into being really affectionate.

30.

Yeah, okay then, I'll give you one about my dad. He was a massive stinge. I had everything hand-me-down from two brothers that were twelve years older than me. I had this bike, which I absolutely loved, and it was a hand-me-down bike. But my brother rode it and broke the back wheel off and it killed me. It was blue as well, because obviously—got given it from a boy. And I think it was already rubbish but yeah, he sat on it, thinking he was clever, rode it and the back wheel came off. I didn't even get another one.

Oh yeah, my dad is meticulous about everything. Everything, including my clothes. Carefully packed away, still smelt like my brother wore them. I remember they had this yellow jumper, like a canary yellow jumper. I don't know why my brother wore that. With a—I don't know what you'd call it—like a rugby collar built into it. And I remember my mum getting it out one day and trying to force me to wear it and I had the type of meltdown that I kill my four-year-old for having. Yeah, I was a boy for quite a long time. I played football. I lived in a little area where there was blocks of houses, not flats, but all the roads were interlinked and I remember a couple of years ago bumping into a guy at the pub that I hadn't seen for years but he's lived near me. He was like, *I remember you—you were that girl who always had the Man U shirt on.* It's not something you wanna hear, is it? I don't really follow football now. Not interested.

31.

In construction, when you put the roof on a building, it's traditional that you have a topping out ceremony. We had got our roof on and we were having our topping out, which was happening in the City Pride, which everyone in Docklands knew—always full of construction.

Our site manager's name was G___. He was an Essex man. He was quite tall, six footish, quite portly, bright red hair, bright red face, for that matter. Fingers like sausages. We're all sitting there in this corner of the pub and G___'s giving his speech and telling us what a good job we've done and all of that. And at this point, I needed the loo. And the only way to get to the loo was to walk through everyone and past G___. So I've gone to do this. I'm walking away from the party and G___ is facing the party. And as I went to pass him, he put his hand out and he grabbed me by the top of my arm, like this. And he wouldn't let me go. We were just standing there. I've got my back to everyone, he's facing everyone. And he's carried on with this speech. And I was getting so embarrassed.

Now here's the thing. At this time I was just in my very, very early twenties and I used to go to the gym like four times a week. So he's holding my arm and what I did was I tensed my muscles in his hand [laughs]. Which nobody else would know this, only G___. And he actually stopped mid-sentence. He turned and looked at me. I looked at him. He released my arm and I went to the loo. And, you know, nobody else ever knew, he never, ever mentioned it.

32.

I find it very difficult to think about the sort of things that I am. When people are describing me I get quite puzzled by some of the stuff they come up with. I put it down to being the middle sibling—that I'm able to lend myself to being different people and letting my personality occupy a comfortable space wherever I am. I grew up with a brother who is a year and a half younger than me and a sister who is just over two years older than me. So we're quite close in age. And I think they knew who they were as people even quite early on. C___'s sensitive, generous, kind and, you know, emotional, melodramatic. And J____ was always just nuts, scary, badly-behaved. I guess you could say that there were two clear identities in who they were as people, good or bad, either side of me. And I think as the middle child you're closer with both of them, in a way that they can't necessarily be as close with each other, just because of the age gap. You're trying to be something to everyone. Or everything to everyone. The only honest answer is that I am a confused mess. I don't think it's the whole *containing multitudes* thing. I don't think that's necessarily true. Everyone can lend themselves to being a slightly different person, in a small way, but people who are the middle sibling would be able to do it with a bit more ease. A bit more willingly as well. I think there's an uncertainty around who I am, and what I might do. That's definitely my own perception. But then, you know, maybe my older sister knows exactly who I am, and either can't articulate it or doesn't want to articulate it because she doesn't care.

33.

By trade I'm a blacksmith. Not many of us now. We work with wrought iron or steel, we can make anything metal—gates, railings, pokers, jewellery, wall art, bracelets. Anything metal. Got my own forge. Do quite a lot of welding. Fabricating. Car repairs. Turn my hand to most things practical, really. Always wanted to do it. Loved it but I went to work instead and then, when I was twenty-two, went to an evening class, fell in love with it, carried on ever since. I've always been into metalwork. It's a form of art that you can do with a hammer. There's a physical side of it and it's artwork. You're bringing cold steel to life, really. I do repairs of old fireplaces, do anything. Anything metal. Bracelets. I've done one for my closest friend and then the rest are mine. I get plenty of jobs just by word of mouth. Keeps me entertained. Keeps me excited. No two jobs are the same.

My grandad had a bull called, what was it called? Mozart! And [the horns] came off when [Mozart] died, about thirty-five years ago. So they're older than me. And they've always been on my grandad's wall in his house. He moved out, he had to go into an old people's home and he was gonna chuck 'em in the skip. So I said, *I'll have them*. Stuck them on the front of me car. Strapped on the front of the car. Yeah, [we're] farmer[s] from generations, all the way, like miles back. Always been in farming. I wouldn't wanna live in the town. I wouldn't wanna live in the city. I couldn't do it. I go there and stay with friends for two or three days and I've had enough.

Street lights and people—it's not my thing. I like darkness and quiet. Much better.

34.

I saw is dogs. Yes. Too many and too big. Two or three. And
they, it is too much hurt me, and then *HOH HOH HOH* like
that. And then I followed the dogs. Across the fields, two big
fields. They are running. They lost behind immediately and
then the small one saved me. That's it. Them saved me. And
then, I just wake up. And I remember the horrible dreams
a couple of years ago—you know, the what-was-name, big
war? Like that, finished, end of the world? Yeah, finished, end
of the world. All people is death and no one living anymore.
I'm scared this one. And then, other people just wake up. All
death people just wake up. Just normal people. And then you
know the volcano, like too much big volcano, all grown up
and I'm scared. Yeah, that dream.

I investigated the meanings. Dog means, if you see dog,
the means, what does it means? Dreams means is sounds
good. Like new jobs, new people, you will see. And then, life
is change, means. Yeah, dogs mean. And other dreams: *You
need to check your life.* And act good people, save people, and
then friendly people. I don't know. Dead mans is nothing good.
But especially, dead mans is when you, real life, not too much
improve. I don't know what happen. I got one more. How can I
say? My wife is gone. Yeah. I cried, too much cry. Yeah. Dream,
dream. And then, wake up, I see my cry. Oh, too much.

Dreams job is my mum. Every night, most of every night,
she say, *I see my dreams,* and I say, *Mum, what's happening?*
and she say, *Be careful. Be careful.*

Mum, come on, say.

No, I can't say. Always be careful.

Every night! Not stopping! Dreams. She is mum. Because too far from me. Every year is one time I see. She miss me. I think so.

What does curiosity look like? I suppose it makes me think of children, so I would probably make it human, if I'm honest. Not in a creepy way, like a child appearing out of nowhere, not like a horror film child, more someone asking questions all of the time. I guess if you're going to extend this weird metaphor then it would be a kid that leads you into interesting places but also potentially risky places. One of the things that I do if I become stressed out or something is think about what my seven-year-old self would say if she saw me now. Usually seven-year-olds think that older people are the boss, so she's always gonna think that it's cool, whatever I'm doing. They're never gonna be disappointed cos they're gonna be like, *Woah, awesome. You're an adult, you do what you want!*

I think about the future of the world a lot more than I did before and it just feels very stressful and impossible to think about without being anxious. So then I think about it less. I worry about things now that I obviously didn't when I was a kid, and they seem really real. And it feels weird to think that I'm gonna go on worrying about them for years and years and years. Rather than it being like when stuff happens at school where you're like, *This is the worst thing that's ever happened to me in my life*, but at the back of your mind you surely know that it's gonna be like a year, or it could even be a week, but then the friendship drama or whatever is over. Whereas now I worry about my parents dying a lot more.

Even though they're not that old. But you never know. And it feels weird to think that that will always be something I'm stressed out about. Until it happens. And then I'll be stressed out about the fact that it happened.

36.

I've stopped and started smoking about four or five times in the last five months. My singing gets really good and I'm like, *I'll do that singing tomorrow when it's really sweet.* And then I'll end up in a situation where I'm five pints in or bumped into someone, end up buying a packet of cigarettes and then back to square one. My friend's always banging on about being in the present. You're trying to be in the moment, and within that moment you're really craving a cigarette. It's gonna keep happening! What happened will keep happening. That's all I've got. I dunno, until we get swallowed up by whatever's coming. Nah, I don't even think like that. If the planet is fucked then it's gonna last longer than us. So maybe it won't keep happening—maybe I take that back. The human race will just be what happened and no more. I heard the plankton's eating the plastic. I know, I don't like to go there but that's what a friend of a scientist friend told me. And that's all you need to think about, really. If the plankton's eating the plastic, that's bottom of the food chain up. Initially you think, *Oh, well I'll stop eating fish.* It doesn't work like that. But there's so much information going out, going round, [sighs] I dunno. It's how you navigate that. That's why I'm interested in actually connecting with people round about me. Something more meaningful like that. You don't have to be best friends with them. It's just that disconnect when you get looking at your phone. I keep calling it your *eyes-on-a-leash*. I'm addicted to it as well. I did three weeks without a phone. It felt weird for a few days—just walking about and not being hooked to what's going on. It was amazing. And then I've gone straight back into it. What happened is I lost my phone and didn't sort it for three weeks and it felt good. And now I'm back! It's like the cigarettes. You'll probably find in ten years it's equivalent [laughs].

I was having this conversation with a friend yesterday, about what sort of people we are, and talking about how we're lovely people, but lovely people don't get anywhere in life. So maybe I don't wanna say I'm a lovely person! We were having this conversation about being long-term single people and that's how we got on to it. You can't put *I'm a nice person* on your Tinder profile because it doesn't achieve anything, saying you're nice doesn't achieve anything. She had an observation once where she was told that she's too lovely to be a teacher, and I think that's such a horrible thing to say, because I don't think anyone can be too lovely. It's nice to be told you're lovely, it's nice to be told you're kind and considerate, and those are the things that I strive in my life to be. That's how I want to be described. They always say nice guys finish last, that's the expression, but we were saying it's nice women as well, nice women always finish last. Being nice doesn't get you a promotion, being nice doesn't get you recognition. And I think that is a terrible, terrible state that we live in if that's the situation.

You're not just one person. You're not always one person. You're multi-levelled as a person. I'm a lovely person, I'm a nice person, I'm a loyal person, that's what I'm like. But then on the other hand I'm an absolute stress-head and I can be an absolute cow. I can get stressed, I can scream and shout, I can cry. I'm a multi-levelled person. It's a very British thing to do, like it's a British thing to queue and say sorry when you walk into people. You don't put yourself at the forefront of things, you think of the negatives, so you can protect yourself. I should say it more often, that I am a lovely person, and I should wear that badge with pride because it should be something I'm proud of. If more people were proud of being lovely, the world would be a better place.

38.

Five years. I come from Somalia, I go Holland like refugee, when I get passport I come here for work. My wife, she live in Holland. Yeah, she still lives in Holland. She don't have passport, that's why. I work here two months, I go there, I come back like this. She can work, she can do everything but she can't come here. She's not allowed, yeah? When I left I was single, I get married in Holland. She is Somalian but she live in Holland.

Smuggler. Smuggler people. Smuggler, they will help me to get me there. I had to pay the money, yeah. Yeah, you cross with fake passport, they will give you in the European. They will take a lot of money. Then they will leave you! Yeah, they will give you the passport, they will let you come, then they will leave you. No, no, to the Holland. Holland. Airplane. More of time, you can't cross, they will know you have fake passport, they pick you up early, you lose your money. Yeah, European passport with someone who looks like you. Because there it's war, it's not peace. Now it's little bit okay but when I was leaving it's very bad. It's very dangerous. Mogadishu. It's a big city. Every time you can see the news—Mogadishu, it's trouble there.

Today my English is very good today! Today it's breathtaking! Normally I don't speak with the people, just say, *Hello!*—it's finished. If I find a lot of people like you my English will be better [laughs]. When I was in Somalia I was doing an English degree—Book One. Book One is like teach you, *Shut the door, What is the boy doing?, How much is the cup of tea?, Please help me.* But when I come here, the people speak very quickly, I don't understand. Just I look the face, I say yes or no.

I have only brother. My mother and my father, they pass. I have only my brother. I am like European now! I live here, I am happy, everything's okay. This is my dream! Here is very expensive. Here is me like paradise.

39.

I'm gonna be thirty-two this year and I'm really coming into
my adult body. Like physically. And I've realised I have to
stop eating bread at every meal! Because I've actually just
started blowing up. And I have to move more, cos I stopped
going to clubs in the same way, I'm not just running on
youthful panic or working every possible moment. So it's
just getting bigger and looser. I can see it happening. I'm still
really attractive. I know what I am. I'm still kind of firm, I
still got quite nice tits. But like, it's all just sort of changing.
I always thought about being in your thirties as like you're
technically an adult. But I am a child. I like nicer wine now
but I'm still a fucking baby [laughs]. I think I've only just
started to feel like an adult. I feel like I'm ten years behind
myself all the time. I feel like I'm only just becoming what I
thought I potentially would be in my twenties. So why don't
I have the banging beach bod to go with? Cos of all the bread
[laughs]. I'm not actually obsessed with being thin either—
that is not [laughs] what I mean. It's just awareness of your
lack of elasticity.

I think when I'm in my fifties I wanna have this third
wind. I think I wanna be sexy, like really glamorously sexy.
I'm gonna be wearing cocktail dresses, I'm gonna be smoking
and I'm gonna be a top shagger [laughs]. But I don't think
I will live very long. I would say I've probably got another
twenty years. Thirty max. I don't wanna upset you, but
we're all gonna die of cancer. The one certainty I think that

all men have is—I mean I'm not a man, so [laughs] that's
reassuring—but the one certainty all men have, really,
is if you don't die by getting hit by a car or murdered or
something, you're gonna die of prostate cancer. I'll probably
die of something smoking-related. Even though I'm not
smoking at the minute, I think I will again, because I know I
want to [laughs]. How else are you supposed to stay fucking
thin [laughs]?

40.

I was nine years old, at my grandmother's house with my cousin. She was two years younger than me and she was a brat. She was extremely spoiled. She would always act up. She was a huge burden on the family. Very much like her mum, who my uncle had married. My younger cousin was from a previous marriage and her mum and her were like two peas in a pod. I just remember them both being a huge burden on the family and a huge issue for my grandparents and my mum and dad, and my other aunts and uncles. And I remember thinking, *One of these days, she's gonna get her comeuppance, I'm gonna see to it.* Because in my eyes, I could see this strain being put on the family and whenever my younger cousin got into trouble, for example, she would just break down, she would say, *I hate you, I hate all of you!* Which is quite strange for a seven-year-old. I remember thinking, *Right, what can I do?*

My grandmother's telephone directory was one of the old-style cases, that you would dial in the letter, and then you would press this long metal bar and it would flip up to the letter, to the surname, and give you your number. And I thought, *If I scratch her name on this metal bar, then she will get an absolute rollocking and it will restore the world to its rightful balance.* And I did it. While I was doing it I remember thinking, *This is genius, this is great.* And then, after a while, I kind of forgot about it.

Then my grandmother found it and absolutely unleashed.

And from that moment, my heart sunk. I felt so sorry for this young girl and to this day I have never spoke to anyone about it. I never spoke to my cousin about it. I mean, I don't see her. My uncle and aunt eventually got divorced and I never ever saw my cousin again after I was about twelve. But it's something that still lives with me today and I still feel extremely bad about it. The only thing that has lived with me that I still feel bad about and I've still never mentioned. Until now.

41.

I've always been scared of water, but abstractly, like I don't like water on my face. I don't think I had anything terrible happen, but I've always felt asthmatic as soon as I get into water. I just was like, *Oh, I'm weak at swimming, I've not really done much swimming with anybody.* I've been swimming in lakes lately, just in the shallows, [and I was] properly wheezing after a few strokes. The people I went with were like, *Jeez, she's really weak.* I just didn't ever push myself, and I accepted the feelings that it brought in me, the warnings, but then I challenged them. And what helped me challenge it was I was with someone that actually couldn't breathe, they have an issue, so I did think, *Whatever this is that happens in water, it's not what she has in water, so maybe it's something I can get past.* And then Friday night I got back from the lake and had a little cry, and I thought, *I'm gonna cross the lake tomorrow.* Which is really out there. It's a big, fuck-off lake. A corner is for being on gliders and stuff, a corner for boats, a corner for giant inflatable slides and stuff. And then swimming through the middle, so it's really big. I don't really set goals and go for them, I just sort of drift.

I took this string with me and I tied it round me with an inflatable, and then I had to convince the people I was with to let me, cos they were like, *Fuck no, you can't swim, you're not crossing the lake!* [Eventually] they were like, *Okay, you've got the ring, you just have lots of breaks in the ring.*

They're very strong swimmers, and I swam across the lake twice as fast as them, with a smile on my face. Wheezing didn't happen. It was gone. It was like the water was lifting me, it was like it was keeping me on the surface and it was with ease. I wasn't tired, I had to wait for them because they were half as slow as me, and then I went back again. It was supernatural. It was very odd. And they were trying to swim but clap, and I could see them as I came onto the shore with my ring that I didn't use [laughs].

42.

I had read the Bible backwards and forwards and when I got to Sunday school, there were a lot of questions. I was like, *Why did he say that? And then do that?* I was a bit like that with people. I just had a lot of questions about where the story came from, where was it published—all these questions. I was asked to leave Sunday school because I asked too many. I was devastated. They just gave me pictures of Jesus to colour in. I'm six and I'd moved on.

Luckily, I realised when I was about eight or nine that it was a story. Very well could've been someone, a true story, but it's a story. Then I relaxed about it. And then I went around like, *I respect all nature and animals and treat the best I can and be respectful and non-judgmental*, and all those things. Which I thought was what they were trying to tell you in the Jesus stories. I used to think, *Well, if I do that, I don't have to go to church. Cos I like roller skating and skateboarding on Sundays.* And also I wasn't good at being quiet. I used to sing too loudly and I used to put my hand up to ask questions! When we went to christenings my mum used to hold my hand down [laughs].

When I was at junior school we had a local church we used to go to and the vicar was definitely fire and brimstone. I used to be terrified. You know: *You're born bad, you can only be good if you do this. And if you don't, this will go on.* That frightened the life out of me. I did become quite obsessed when I was younger, first of all that God was watching me, and then I thought Jesus might be watching me. And I got quite upset about it all. I had to get to grips with what it was all about. Because I also believed in fairies. And I decided one day that I did believe in fairies more than God and Jesus. And then I was sorted. It's what you choose to see as fact. I stand by believing in fairies to this day. I'm with it all the way [laughs]. I'm not letting go of them! I'm not gonna let go of that one. That's my saving grace.

43.

Depression hit me out of nowhere when I was twenty-seven. I didn't know what was causing it. In regards to home life, relationship, job—there were ticks in a lot of the boxes. And I couldn't understand what it was. It was down to me being stagnant in life. For the past decade, I'd been stuck in a box. Not even a box, a raft, just going with the current of life. Getting promotions at work and certain things happening but not realising that it was not really any of my doing in regards to me actually making something happen. It was just stuff that happened along the way in the raft.

At that time I was feeling suicidal but it ain't like I was gonna take action and take my own life. It was just I was feeling low. Life was a bit long. I found out, two years after, that suicide was the leading cause of death in males under the age of forty-five. When I was going through what I was going through, that was such a large burden for me. And I just thought how many things are there that us as men carry as burdens? Because, you know, not speaking for every man, but we don't tend to be open, share, have conversations. I think for a lot of men their journey in life has been a very solo journey. A lot of adversity, or things that they've faced or come up against, have been faced alone. So it's just normalising a lot of the things and actually saying that there's benefits in doing certain stuff and then people just realising that *I'm not alone*.

I think a lot of men haven't got circles where they're able to be entirely authentic, real. Men tend to banter and take the mick out of each other a lot of the time, so then naturally to be vulnerable, there may be a backlash that comes from that. Also, in relationships, they feel that they have to take on this role of being the man and the protector, and being strong. And then I guess in the majority of households around the world, in the UK also, there's some sort of dysfunction. There's some sort of issue, whether it's dealing with alcohol issues, mental health, sexual abuse, but there's some sort of dysfunction in a lot of households. A lot of stuff is held within. Everybody has a poker face on in regards to life, really.

44.

It got taken up by the punk rockers, and that's where I came
into it. Because it was 1980 and all the kids who were older
than me, the white kids were in punk rock bands and the kids
of Jamaican descent had reggae bands. So that kind of moulded
together. And it worked, you know. Also, the words of that
time were still about rebellion and alienation and smoking
herb. And that's what you do when you're a teenager, innit?

That's where I started, just by buying records, rather
than anything else. I was at school, about fourteen. North
London, Camden Town. So I was always in Camden Market
and Camden Record & Tape Exchange. I went to school in
Cricklewood so I would cross town. We used to go trawling
through Notting Hill and Shepherd's Bush, all the record
shops down there. Travelling around town was something
that I did a lot of, which was just wonderful. You know, out
on the Red Bus Rovers just buying records. One time I was
waiting for the 52 bus and I had this amazing record, which
was really rare, it was called 'Tell Me That You Love Me'
by Trevor Byfield. And the 52 came and the bus driver just
looked me in the eyes, I was sticking my arm out, he looked
me in the eye and he kind of laughed and drove straight past.
I got so annoyed I threw my bag on the floor. And I smashed
the record. Terrible. On Ladbroke Grove. I bought the reissue,
of course, a couple of years ago. It's got early scratching
on the B side, it's great. I think it's not scratching, it's just
someone doing the tape machine, but same sound, really.

Dub is about the revolution of form, isn't it? It's about where you have a song that is completely formed in one way, then you completely upset the way it evolves and you make an alien version of that. It is a remix, but it's a more traditional kind of idea, one that kind of upends the form and frames it completely different. It's almost like looking at a photograph in negative. And in fact, it's even more radical. It's one of those where you draw on the negative and all that kind of shit. The mystery of it was always so exciting. You had to seek out the different versions and then trace where things came from. The otherness of it was always so exciting. It became a kind of quest for me.

45.

I think it's just that idea of being able to have a nap. I love having naps in the middle of the day, to be really honest—usually frowned upon in the workspace to do that [laughs]. I find being able to take my time very satisfying. This idea of not having to live by a clock, or have to be somewhere at a certain time. I'm somebody who maybe needs to take her time a little bit more on certain days, or certain things. There's a satisfaction in knowing that I don't operate on somebody else's timeframe or schedule. Even to be able to take ten-minute chunks of the day, to pause, or stop looking at a screen and just stretch—those kind of really basic things. I'm hearing myself say this and it makes me also a little bit angry. [It] feels like such a revolutionary thing in a way, taking a break. A fifteen-minute break from work is frowned upon because you're not operating at maximum productivity levels. Even if you would be genuinely much better off taking that break and then coming back refreshed and focusing. I'm half Middle Eastern and half French as well, so I grew up with, *Lunch is an hour and you go outside and you go out for nice food at a bistro or a small restaurant.* Here, it's a sandwich at your desk. It's not the same, it's just not the same.

I think it's this idea of reclaiming something. This idea that you've gotten away with something, but kind of small, mischievous [laughs]. That kind of little stolen moment that you carve out for yourself, and you're like, *Mmmmm.*

Something quite personal, enjoyable. I really like to go swimming and I feel very satisfied when I can cut the day in half and go for a swim and then come back. I'll be doing the exact same amount of work that I would be on a normal day but knowing I've had that little moment for myself in the middle of the day, that nobody really knows about, is quite satisfying [laughs]. You did something that you would not normally allow yourself to do, and it means that it's something you keep close to your heart, and you don't necessarily want to share with others.

I've had a nap at 11 a.m.! When you've had a hard morning and you feel like, *Oh, didn't wake up on the right side of the bed today*, then an 11 a.m. nap and you're like, *Okay, still early enough in the day to start over!*

46.

I've got a migraine which I've had for five and a half years now. And it just refuses to go away. So it's a bit of a pain and a bit of a nuisance. For quite a long time, I was on quite a lot of painkillers. I was also on morphine for about a year, which I don't recommend to anyone. Cold turkey is nowhere near as fun as the name suggests. You'd be amazed how much sweat comes off your legs, actually. Awful kind of worrying [laughs]. But that's another story.

I could smell things and I couldn't work out what it was I was smelling. I had a headache that just wouldn't go away. It turns out I was smelling dyes. We had a couch delivered and I couldn't go anywhere near it for about a month because I could smell the dye. I can smell copper. I get phantom smells, things that no one else can smell. It's like the world's worst superpower. Absolutely useless and pointless. We're still trying to figure out what it is but it's migraine-related. It just sort of sits, it's like a constant pain in one part of my head that refuses to go away, but every so often, I can only describe it like a child walking past a hi-fi as it's playing and just whacking the volume up very quickly—*AAARGH!* So it means regular work is out the window. My hobby turned into my job. I had a little hobby tape label, which is now a fully fledged tape label.

I do all the duplication. I've got a bank of fancy tape decks which I've managed to get for cheap, which allow me to record two things at once in real time, so the quality's better.

I can do a run of a hundred in about a week. So technically I can turn out a tape a week, sort of thing. There was one last week. There was two out the week before. This one might be next week, actually. I'm still waiting for the covers. It was never done to make money. I don't do things for the money. I refuse to cash in, sort of thing. I've never done anything for money. I do it because I want to. And obviously because I enjoy it. And there's something quite, I dunno, it's quite relaxing just getting the tapes and putting them all in. I get the labels printed locally, and the covers. It's quite nice, is that. They're all hand-assembled. Some of the labels are on slightly wonky. You wouldn't get that with a machine.

47.

In the last three years I've had memories of something that
I didn't remember at all, didn't know about. My body kept
this thing secret from me for forty years. I went to see the
film *Memento*, accidentally, some time ago, or when it came
out. And he has these flashbacks to possibly killing his wife.
In the film there are these moments when it's like electric
lightning round his scalp and that's what it feels like, having
these memories come back. And at one point, when I'd had
these memories that made me realise I didn't know my own
past, I was scared that a memory might come of me doing
something similar. Like murder. I don't believe that anymore.
I don't think I've ever murdered anyone, but I genuinely
thought I might've murdered someone for a while.

The memories are of myself being sexually abused
between the ages of around four and ten. And it is a secret in
a way, because there are people I need to protect, so although
I've told friends and family, I don't feel able to make it public.
And I suppose I also feel some weird shame—the shame that
you feel at having someone treat your body in a way which
is like you are not a person. That's the shame that I feel, or
that I sometimes feel, and then sometimes I forget, or I feel
something different.

So what kind of secret is it? My body hid knowledge that
this happened. I'm pretty sure it happened. But I won't ever
know for sure exactly what it was that happened, or didn't
happen—in my grandparents' garden, my grandparents'

spare bedroom, the park, our house. I don't know. It's a secret, still—whether it happened, or exactly what happened, and what the sensations in my body are and what the terror is about. It's a secret from myself.

And it shouldn't be a fucking secret. You wanted the quotidian, and I think this is. I think it's everyday, *every day*. It happened to me more often than I could imagine and it happens to little children more often than we can imagine, or bear to think about. So it's everyday. It shouldn't be a secret, and in some ways it's not a secret. We all know, but there's nothing we can fucking do about it. I don't know if this is what you want. But weirdly, I suddenly took this opportunity to talk to you about it and I don't know if the secret is sexual abuse, or rape, or becoming somebody who has strange memories in a strange way. Maybe my secret is that I'm one of those people who's had a weird, mystical experience of memories leaking back.

My dad came here in the seventies and then I was born in
Bangladesh and we all moved here when I was just first born,
which was 1982. He started working in kitchens when he
came over here and then he started his own business, just a
few years after I was born. I was raised up here and then I
spent a bit of time in London, did my A levels in London and
my degree in London, but came back here to run the family
business, which is an Indian restaurant. It closed in 2016, but
I was running that for about five years, I think. I had started
a family so it's best that I don't do those longish hours
anymore, so I work for the government now.

It's funny we're talking now, because I'm actually heavily
involved in a group here called the Black Lives Matter Jersey
group. Basically, we held a sort of protesting event, and there
were a lot more people than we thought, than we anticipated.
We're in the early stages of the group and we're trying to
move things forward regarding getting statues taken down—
because Jersey's got a history of colonialism and slaves as well,
so we're petitioning to get statues taken down. We're looking
at equal pay for those people from Africa who have come to
work in accountancy firms and for our hospital and private
clinics etcetera. I'm gonna try my best to organise an event,
possibly a music event here as well. Obviously taking place
next year rather than this year.

Being involved in this group is exposing me to other
cultures and people that are struggling somewhere here

in Jersey. There were a couple of Black speakers who were talking about how they were racially abused here in Jersey. And also being a Muslim as well, thankfully it's not happened to me and it's not happened to my wife even though she's a hijabi, but I've heard that people from our mosque were abused as well, being insulted and stuff like that, being called all sorts of slurs. But yeah, the weird things is—and I guess I need to touch wood here—I've not experienced it in my many years of being here.

We've got a mosque here and we manage to fill it—well, we used to be able to fill it every Friday when we do our Friday congregation prayers. I would say it goes up to around about sixty for those Friday prayers but I wouldn't actually know what the number is regarding number of Muslims in Jersey. I don't know what the population is. But, as you can imagine with every part of the UK, there's a number of Indian restaurants, so there's some Bangladeshis just like us that run the restaurants.

I normally do it on beaches. I do it in Margate, at Bournemouth, sometimes in Dover. It's my hobby and I love finding treasures and ancient stuff and plus it makes me walk a lot without me realising. Which is a good thing on the beach as well. I keep myself busy with things like that. Away from any other things. Beach time, we go to the beach and get the metal detector and I got a couple of people coming to me, say, *I lost a ring can you give a sweep?* It's a good hobby. I got quite a good metal detector. It can differentiate between gold, silver, metal. Make a different noise and it gives you a picture on a screen as well. It's a very professional one. That one cost me about one thousand and a half. So you don't look for irons and scrap, things like that. You only set it up on platinum, gold, silver, jewellery. I've set it up so gold sound, it become a really faded, old sound. And silver is more of a clear sound. Iron is more of a clicking sound so you just ignore it—you don't have to dig up every single target otherwise you'd be digging for years. The main target is walk along with it and spend some more time on the hobby as well.

To be honest, I found a very nice gold ring. Twenty-two carat. Normally when I find stuff I try to see if there is any names or addresses, to give it back to the family. Cos if I lost something and someone give it back to me that means a lot. This one didn't have anything. It only say twenty-two carats. It's a very big one as well and it's got precious stone with it as well. I didn't even check it, to be honest. I still have it with other finds at home. You find glasses, you find coins. I found very old jewelleries. I find very old coins, like when you look at them and it says 1940, 1910.

I love archaeologies and things like that, watching ancient Egypt and things like that. And I think long ago they found two ancient skeleton in Nottingham. There is like a mountain and it's got a door in. They were just doing the pavement and one of the workers, he dug down around two metres and he thought it was a pipe and when he cracked it, it was actually a skull. They called the police and the police came on the scene and they said, *This is not a murder scene.* They were about two thousand years old. I think they were Roman skeletons or something.

I've been here since 2003. Just after the war in Iraq. We're from Mosul. The city called Mosul.

50.

The kids were very young. I got up one morning and I was driving to work, and I suppose I no longer knew which way I was supposed to be going? I felt like, *I'm gonna get to work and I'm gonna get grief and hassle and I'm gonna get grief and hassle when I get home because I've not been at home.* And I felt that I needed to be at home rather than at work. So I handed my resignation in. I said to my wife, *I'm gonna take six months and then I'll find another job.* And that six months turned into three years looking after the kids.

My wife said to me, *If you're stopping work I want a new kitchen and you can fit it.* And some of L___'s colleagues from work came round for drinks or something and they were admiring the kitchen and L___ just happened to say I did it. And they went, *Oh, will he do ours?* So the long and short of it was I started fitting kitchens and bathrooms for people, just word of mouth.

I did a house in L____ and I was there for quite a long time because I did two bathrooms and a kitchen for this lady, whose mum then asked me to do very similar at her house, so I got to know the family really well. They were from French Guiana. One afternoon I was there and she said, *Look, I'm cooking, why don't you have some food?* And this food was fantastic. So I said to her, *You must let me have the recipe.* She said, *I'll show you how to make it.* From then on, part of my charge for doing your bathroom or your kitchen was you taught me how to cook your favourite dish. And I'd got the intention of actually putting a cookbook together, of these random people's favourite meals. But I ended up going back to a proper job!

To be honest, the very first one is the only one that I regularly do. And I've passed on that recipe to numerous people. I don't know how to describe it, it was some sort of curried lamb, I suppose. Incredibly hot. So it was just basically onions cooked in sugar and caramelised, almost to the point of being black. And then I think it was nutmeg went in and garlic and soy sauce. And the meat was just sprinkled with chilli flakes. And you leave those for an hour or so and then you put them into the onion and that soy mix and then cover with water and then just let that cook down. It's not complicated but when I first had it at her house, it was fiery hot. She said her husband likes it a lot hotter, *But I've toned it down for you and my kids!*

51.

I need to see where I'm going to be able to head for it. If
I don't have that motivation then I struggle. When I get
thrown off of my goal, I go into a little bit of a panic then
cos I don't know where I'm heading. So that's what I've been
doing, manically, for the past three weeks. I've been sitting
down and mind-mapping my interests—which ones would
benefit me in the long term, which ones would provide
a successful career. I've always had a plan but it's always
changed! I wanted to be a nurse at one point in my life.
That was even not that long ago. And I had a clear pathway:
I was able to transfer to a nursing degree without doing a
foundation year, and I had the university and I'd emailed
lecturers, and it was all sorted. And then I changed my mind
[laughs]. Then I was interested in doing business and perhaps
marketing. And then I changed my mind! It's not that I don't
have an interest in these roles, but it's more that I don't get
excited by it. I think I'd be good at them, but whether or not
I'd enjoy doing it, I'm not sure.

I believe in the law of attraction. If I want something, I've
got to know what I want for it to happen to me. It sounds
really silly but I'm a big believer in vision boards and that
sort of thing. It's basically arts and crafts. I just get a big
piece of card, A3 size, and I'll sit down and ask myself loads
of questions—*What do I want from the future? Where do I
see myself in five years? What sort of job? Where will I be
living?* And I find photos or write it down and lay it all out

and make it look nice and pretty, and then that's it. It's in my room and I look at it every day and I've got that vision every morning when I wake up, and I know why I'm going to college, and why I'm working hard that day. I think if you write it down and you have a clear pathway and a clear goal, you are much more likely to actually get it. Rather than just saying, *Oh I'd like to do this one day* and never actually sitting down and really working towards it. I think if you have a clear goal and a clear end point, you're much more likely to get there. I very much think that if your subconscious isn't on board you're not gonna be on board. And it can take a lot of time to actually get in sync with your subconscious. So I think having a clear goal and having that imagery in the back of your head can definitely help you get there. You need to have every part of you on board.

52.

I've grown up in Sunderland, in the North East, so first hand seen quite a lot of the impact of government policy that's not very inclusive of my region. That's putting it nicely! I'd always lived in Sunderland and I have family in Scarborough, which is another prime example of these areas that have been negatively impacted by the past century's worth of politics. But, other than that, I didn't really go into any other cities until I started sixth form and I started going to Newcastle—just because I fancied a change of scenery, just because the sixth forms in Sunderland didn't really sound as good. And that was when I really started getting into politics as well, at the start of sixth form. I'd make the hour and a half journey into Newcastle every day, and spending every day in Newcastle makes me realise, *Oh, hang on, there's bigger cities out there that aren't even that far away from me.*

It was then when I started realising it's not just a coincidence that Newcastle's a nicer city—it all comes down to the funding, cos it's the only area in the North East that gets any sort of attention from the government. And moving down to Manchester made me realise that even further. It makes me look back at my life in Sunderland and think, *Okay, what major construction projects has there been?* Not really many. It's just an endless cycle of the buildings getting knocked down to make car parks. It's a running joke in my family, the car parks. It just got me thinking, you know.

And the problem is how do you explain this to a middle-class family in London who have watched their city get built up and up and up, and who maybe don't ever have the need to go to the North East? Who don't come to my region and other regions like it? You've got places like Burnley and Yorkshire—all across the country really. So long as they're shielded from that they're not gonna want to change anything, cos it doesn't affect them. I guess a lot more social equality is the underpinning. And that comes through crushing the boundaries between race, between religion, between social status. For me, it all comes down to equality. But it's just the realism of achieving that [sighs]. It's not a really achievable thing in my eyes. In the short term, anyway. It's a tough one.

Only thing I can think to add would be Sunderland back in the Premier League [laughs]. It's so important for the people round here. It's so, so important, the football, and for a lot of people it's the one refuge they've got from working a nine till five—you go out on the weekend, you go watch the football, and it's such a huge part of the city's culture. And it's just sad to watch it get rotted away. We've been living off hope for the last twenty years.

I was twenty-three, twenty-four, living in South London.
I was at university—well, art college—and I hadn't seen
my dad for a number of years—maybe two, I think, maybe
three. I can't remember now. Anyway. I got a phone call one
morning, from my stepmum, who never calls me, so I picked
it up straight away. I said hello and she said, *I'm terribly
sorry to tell you that your father's had a heart attack and he
happens to be in London and he's been rushed to [hospital].
Can you go over there?* Because she wasn't anywhere near
town, anywhere near London. So I said okay. I was the only
person in my family in London at the time. My sisters were
both at university elsewhere. I rushed over to *[the hospital]*,
and my dad was, yes, in critical condition.

I ran up to whatever floor it was—I think it was floor 4,
floor 5, something like that—and asked to find out where he
was and just as I was asking a nurse, he got wheeled past me
on a hospital bed, tubes in and out of him and everything
else. He was about to go into theatre. And the woman
explained that he was gonna need a triple bypass and that
this could be the last time I'd ever see him. And she asked
me if I had anything I wanted to say. I paused and looked at
him and said no, I didn't have anything left to say to him.
Partly cos I couldn't think of anything but also because it
would've felt insincere and cheap, I think.

Anyway, he went into the operating theatre and for the
next couple of hours I assumed he was gonna die—cos you

know, triple bypass, I've been told he's got like a 5 per cent chance of making the surgery blah blah blah. I'm outside on the riverside bit in that garden, very upset and confused. I was confused as to why I was upset. I thought I didn't like him and then suddenly I'm grieving for him and it was a very confusing time. I went through the whole gamut of emotions, from anger to denial to grief to crying, thinking about the future. I imagined my entire future without my dad. I was gonna dedicate my last art project to him, I was gonna then have to get a job to look after my half-sister, all this sort of stuff.

To cut a long story short, he recovered. And at the time he recovered, I actually wished he hadn't recovered, because it made everything far more complicated, him actually staying alive. And all of this new life I'd imagined seemed so much more attractive to me, and so much more a place where I could exist outside of his presence and outside of his influence, and kind of ascend to his position of authority in the family. So when I first saw him in the hospital and he was smiling and saying, *Hi, I've survived*, I pretended I was happy, but actually I wasn't.

My grandmother [died] when I was two. Obviously really
sad—she was only fifty-six and left my grandpa, my dad's
dad, left him completely heartbroken. She was the love of his
life. She was, by all accounts, quite a wonderful woman, from
what I can gather. I was the only grandchild at that time.
Because he'd lost her, my mum and dad basically wanted him
to have me as a bit of a distraction. So I used to go and stay
with my grandpa from when I was really, really young. So
as a result of my grandmother's death, I actually ended up
having a really, really close relationship with my grandpa. I
have these most amazing memories of my grandfather as a
result of that. I always used to sleep in this double bed in his
spare room, and he used to put me to bed and then sit there
and just wax lyrical for hours about his time in India and
his life and my grandmother and how they met. He had this
really wild personality and imagination.

He was also a really snappy dresser. He always used to be
absolutely immaculately turned out, not a hair out of place.
He used to go and have his nails done, his hair done. Loved
shopping and actually loved shopping for me. Even from
being very young, when I used to stay with him, he used
to take me shopping and I could choose whatever I wanted.
Much to my mum's disgust! He'd want to buy me a full
outfit—shoes, the whole shebang. It was like a showing—
he'd like to see all the options, he'd have to see everything.
I remember I had this absolutely hideous lurid, bright pink

dress from C&A with frills and bows. And my mum was quite cool. She'd bought me OshKosh B'gosh dungarees and stuff to be a cool child and I wanted to wear this lurid pink dress. Mum would just be like, [mouths] *What the fuck is that?!*

He actually ended up getting Alzheimer's in his old age. But I think he always sort of had that—he was always really eccentric and talked too much. He was a bit mad. And just got more and more honest as he got older. I remember my cousin went to see him before he died. I think it was when I was pregnant, cos I was actually pregnant with my little boy when he died. And she said, *Oh, you know __'s pregnant?* And he said, *Oh yes, I know. She's my favourite, you know* [laughs]. She's like, *Oh yeah, we know, Grandpa!* He just didn't care by this point. My cousin R_____, her husband has got the same birthday as me and one year—this was probably about ten years ago—[Grandpa] sent [him] a birthday card with a picture of me in it [laughs]. Like, a photograph of me! And R_____ rang him, like, *Thanks for [my husband]'s card but why've you sent him a picture of __?* He was just like, *Oh well, I thought he might want to remember what she looks like. I mean, she is very beautiful.*

55.

There's a quote that I really like and I can't remember who
it's by, but it's by a snooty foreigner who said that the
English don't like music, they just like the noise it makes.
I think that completely describes my relationship with
music. I have no understanding of music but I do like the
noise it makes. And I feel the same about photography. I
don't understand photography in the way that a university-
educated person might, but I like the way it looks, and I don't
think that's a flippant thing to say about either of them,
actually. The thing I like most about music is its timbres—it's
the textures, it's the surfaces, it's the way that this incredibly
abstract art form can change your state of mind and get you
into worlds that don't exist. Just a load of waveforms in the
ether. And exactly the same is true of photography, whether
it be abstract or not—patterns on a screen or a piece of paper,
textures and colours and things that are not that dissimilar
from sounds can get you into a space that nothing else can.

One of the things I say about photography is that if it's
not better than being there, it's not worth it. So if it's just a
record of an instant, if you'd been there you would've seen
that. Fine, great, there's a place for that. But photography
at its finest is when it adds something that kind of wasn't
there—although obviously it was there cos it's just a
photograph. When you put things in a frame, when you cut
around experience, that makes it different. It's about the
totality in a way, isn't it? That everything in that picture is

meant to be there. In the same way that everything in a piece of music is meant to be there, even if it's improvised and there's accidents and all the rest of it. There's still a reason why those fluffed notes are there and that's part of it. And the same for photography. It's absolutely fine for it to be messy round the edges, or wonky, or whatever. It's an editing process.

In a photograph, or in a piece of music, all well-created textures are beautiful. You can take a photograph of something horrible and you can make it beautiful through the textures, and the same is true of music. You can get some really harsh, horrible sounds and you can mash them together in some horrible ways, and it has a beauty. And if you can hold the space, as it were, then you can enjoy and appreciate the texture of any photograph—any good photograph, whatever that means. And I guess, if you wanted to be philosophical, you could say the same thing about life, although obviously it's an awful lot harder when it's punching you in the face and it hurts than when it's a piece of paper, or some wave forms. But there is a beauty to all of it, even the stuff that really seems like it isn't. Although I think that's too facile a thing to say, you see what I mean? Tell that to a grieving mother. I mean, come on.

56.

I'm almost thirty-five and I feel like I still don't really know
what's going on with sex. When we were at school there was
no concept of consent or respect or anything like that. It was
reduced to biology, wasn't it? If you have sex with someone
you might get pregnant or you might get an STD and that's
it. I don't think we were really given much guidance on the
emotional complexity of sex. And I think I'm still kind of
confused by that, years and years later. I would love it if I
could say that I've felt intimate with, or felt safe with, or
trusted everyone that I had sex with. But there was definitely
a phase when I was in my early twenties, when I was just
baffled by life in general, where I think that I actively looked
for people that I knew I didn't want to have a relationship
with. That I knew I wouldn't invest too heavily in [or] fall
in love with. And those are the people that I was having sex
with. Because there's less at stake, I guess. [And] the people
that I fell in love with weren't the people I was having sex
with. Does that make sense? That sounds really bizarre,
doesn't it?

I think a big part of that comes from the sort of Victorian
basis of our education system and the church and things like
that, which associate sex with shame. [The] residue of that
is that I don't think we're very in touch with ourselves. And
so it takes all this time to figure it out. And then you get this
sort of melting pot of hormones and bodies and emotions
and, added to the mix, modern society and technology and

all these things. And personally, I think that's resulted in me feeling really confused for a lot of my sexual adult life.

I think around the time when I first started feeling the confidence to take control of my sexuality was probably when I got into a relationship with my current partner. He's the first man that I have always trusted and always felt really safe with. I think that's why we're still together. And so I think he was the first person that I really associated [with] intimacy and sex and safety and all these things which you want to bring together. I think he was the first person that I did that with. But then I had kids! And kids really throw a spanner in the works for your sex lives. Once they start sleeping, I might have the space to explore that kind of level of agency, d'you know what I mean? But I quite like the fact that I'm thirty-five and I still feel like I'm young in terms of my sex life. I don't wanna think that because I'm not in my twenties anymore, it's all over. Or like, because I'm with a long-term partner that that's the end. We can't be complacent and be like, *Right, I'm with this person now, that's it*. It has to be an ongoing process. I mean, I'm saying this now, but it's also kind of a revelation for me, because I don't think I have the mental headspace in my everyday life to dwell on these things, although talking about them I feel like they're important.

Sorry, I can see the baby stirring.

57.

I've always been the sort of person who thinks about life in a straight line, planning everything out. Following the crowd, I suppose—following what people would say is the normal thing. You know, graduating, buying a house, getting a dog, getting married, all that. And then obviously after getting married, trying to think about having a child, having a family. I've always been healthy as well—I run a lot, I like my fitness, never really had any health problems. But then when it came to trying to start a family I got seriously ill. And after a year from hell, I got diagnosed with a condition called endometriosis. It's a condition that one in ten women across the world have. I'd never even heard of it. And from there it's been a tough year, and a lot has happened, a hell of a lot has happened. I thought it was gonna be a mild condition. I'm having major surgery in a couple of weeks now. I've lost a whole kidney, I've lost kidney function, I'm having the bladder removed. I've been really lucky in life, I've had such a nice upbringing, I've succeeded in my career, found my husband, and then having something like that happen to your health at thirty years old was a massive knock.

I try and speak a lot about the condition to raise awareness. It's a chronic condition and I've had it since I was thirteen years old, but it's gradually gotten worse over time. They have said to me if I would have been diagnosed and found out about the condition ten years ago then I wouldn't have lost my kidney function and I wouldn't be facing the six-hour surgery that I'm going to be facing. And then obviously again the coronavirus was another setback. It was one of those where the operation was cancelled and I didn't hear anything for ten weeks, so I had no idea what was gonna happen. The treatment I have to take means that I'm not able to have a child at the moment and to start a family. I have good days but then I have days on end where I can't get out of bed, I'm in so much pain and agony with the condition. I can't get out of bed and I can't eat for seventy-two hours, I can't sleep for seventy-two hours, and it really has had a huge impact on my life.

Once I'd come to terms with it, opening up about it helped a lot. You realise how brilliant other people are—being there for you and comforting you, and also just treating you as normal as well. I think I was a bit worried about people looking at me differently, or being more mindful of me, especially with child-type things, cos a lot of my friends are having children now. The last thing I wanted was for them to feel they can't tell me they're pregnant cos they might upset me, or they're worried about me meeting the baby in case I'd cry holding a baby, or that sort of thing. But they haven't been like that at all, and it hasn't been like that at all for me, either.

D'you know what the strange thing is as well? Even when I talk about it to people, it's like I'm talking about someone else's life. It's so strange. Some days it doesn't even feel real that it's happening to me.

58.

My sister is a massive extrovert. She works in psychology
and she did one of those personality tests, and they rank you
on a number of attributes, and for the extroversion one she
got 99 per cent. Which apparently is unheard of. For her, she
needs to go out—she needs to go clubbing and go to bars and
stuff, and if she doesn't have that, which she didn't have for
the last few months, she doesn't feel like herself. She doesn't
feel like a full human, and her mental health suffers because
of that. Whereas I found that I personally don't need that at
all. I'm trying to think what my equivalents are of needs that
make me feel like me. I suppose I need alone-time to reflect.
Since I was a kid, I kept a journal, and I never felt like things
had actually happened until I wrote it down in that journal.
I needed that reflection time to make it feel like an event,
like it happened, and I suppose that was a need. Where does
the barrier of need and compulsion stop? For my sister, for
example, if she had to go out every night, clubbing, to feel
like she was real, people would look at that and say, *Hmm,
that's a bit of an issue* [laughs]. And I wonder if you could
say the same about needing to write things down all the time,
to process them, whether that's compulsion as well? I feel
like I'm a bit untethered, a bit ungrounded, if I haven't done
it for a while, but I kind of stopped. I tailed off a bit during
lockdown, because nothing was happening [laughs]. Since I
started working, I slowed down. Maybe it's cos I'm busier,
maybe it's because I don't find what I'm doing as interesting

anymore, worth writing down? I don't feel like I know who I am. But then, if I re-read journal entries, I don't recognise that person as me either.

We're twins, did I mention that? So yeah, she's my twin sister but I never call her my twin, just because I feel like she's my sister. Yeah, very different. I've watched videos of us when we were two or three, and our personalities are already defined, they're already quite concrete. She dazzles when she goes into a room—she's a bit wild, is how she would describe herself [laughs]. I think she would say that she was attention-seeking, but I just see it as she's really fun, really lively and very vivacious. It's funny, my friends who don't know my sister think that I'm extroverted, and that I'm quite bubbly and lively, but I never see myself that way, because I always see myself compared to what she is. So I would describe myself as introverted and almost reserved.

It's hard to know where our personalities start and begin, and how much of it is defined against the other person. I would imagine if she was to choose ten words to describe herself, there would be words that most people would put on that list that she wouldn't put on, because I have those attributes, and she sees them as me. So I'm the sensible one, that's how we both see me. And then there's the line in between—how much am I naturally sensible and how much [have] I had to be sensible to look after my wild sister [laughs]? Maybe that's my need. I need to feel like I'm looking after someone, so she supports that need!

The secret I want to share is one that I have kept for fifty years and it dates back to when I was at junior school.

There were two characteristics I had in those days. One was that I was very, very fond of war and battles, especially medieval war and battles. I thought the idea of the knight in armour was a really romantic concept, I was really into that. I had lots of toy soldiers who were knights in armour, that kind of thing. And the other thing: I very much liked poetry. I liked jingly, rhyming verse, that was the kind of poetry I liked. And one day I found something in my older sister's annual. It was an annual from a comic which I think barely anyone remembers now, it was called *Girls' Crystal*, the *Girls' Crystal* annual. And in that, along with all the comic strips and the stories and so forth, there was a little poem. And this poem—actually I say little, it was quite long, like a page long, with illustrations—combined my two loves because it was a poem and it was about a knight in armour. I still remember how it began. It went, *Sir Timothy Tinribs, the knightliest knight / Was questing around for a dragon to fight.* It was all about the exploits of this rather comic character, but also very brave, valiant knight in armour, Timothy Tinribs, who fights this dragon and saves a damsel in distress. It really stuck in my mind and I found, without really meaning to, that I had memorised it.

The following week in school, we were asked to write a poem. And I had this one at my fingertips. I was able to copy it out line by line and present it as my own work. And the teacher, Mrs ____ , was really quite taken aback by how long it was, and how perfectly it scanned and rhymed, and the humour of it. She thought it was brilliant. She said, *Did you copy this from somewhere?* And I said, *No, no. I mean, where could I have copied it from?* And, certainly, there was nothing in the classroom that I could've copied it from. I think she found it difficult to believe that I could've memorised such a long poem like that. *Very good, gold star*, etcetera.

The next thing I heard, they wanted to put it in the school magazine. I lived in terror for a while in case my sister recognised it and said, *Hey, that comes from my annual!* But she never did. I don't think she ever read the school magazine. My dad was really, really impressed and he would show it to everybody, when people would come round, when neighbours would come round. He'd say, *Look, look, look at this poem ____'s got in the school magazine.* My mother never said much about it and she actually was a teacher at the school. And I'm pretty sure, looking back, that she suspected, or that she knew, in fact. But she never exposed me. She let me get away with it. And so I got this name of being a brilliant poet, and people used to come up to me in the playground and ask me to make up rhymes for them. I hugged that secret to myself for a long, long time, as I say for about fifty years, and I now feel that I can unburden myself of it. So I'm just gonna admit that Sir Timothy Tinribs was a shameless piece of plagiarism.

60.

It's something to do with social conscience. It's something to do with concern for others. In today's world—I suppose it's always been the same—the people who have little concern for others tend to be the ones who dominate the media and dominate the news. And that disturbs my peace of mind [laughs], is the best way to put it. I would like to see more people find and display and act on their social conscience— assuming they have one. I think a lot of people do, but they just don't know it. Y'know, because of the way we live.

I didn't know it. I had a very conventional life. Grew up in a normal family, studied at university, got a job, developed a career, and everything was very tickety-boo. No issues. Everything went very smoothly, very well. But I wasn't exposed to the wider world. I wasn't exposed to people and groups of people who didn't have the same sort of advantages that I had in life. And then I started to get involved with people who had had very different life experiences and were having very different life experiences. And it was only when I became exposed to those people, and engaged with them and worked with them, that I started to develop some understanding of what a social conscience meant, and how it might affect things. It's just exposure. I didn't know there were all these worlds outside my own little world. Up until that point I didn't have a social conscience that manifested itself in any way, other than personal relationships. Beyond that there was nothing. I didn't know what social conscience meant.

I suppose I would feel more peace of mind if I saw more of that in the world at large. Even if—to just take it a step further—if I saw more attempts by society in general to facilitate the development and manifestation and application of people's social consciences. It's left too much to individuals and charitable organisations and all the rest of it to try and drive it. There should be a bit more power behind it somewhere. It has to be based on changing individual views and education must play a part in that, from a young age. I think we do tend to live in our own little worlds, without being exposed. We read about things in the news and see things on TV or social media or whatever, but whenever you actually get close to something and you see it and feel it, you can touch it, I think it has more impact than simply seeing it on a screen or on a bit of paper or whatever. So education, exposure, would be parts of it. That is, if such a thing is possible. Y'know, is the nature of mankind what it is? And will it always be thus?

I don't think it has to be radical. I don't think it has to be a full-time job, trying to manifest it. It might be you influence little things here and there, or just simply influence the way somebody else thinks. As long as you're doing something, however major or minor that happens to be. But something. Because I think at the end of the day, lots of little things can add up to a lot more than one big thing. So as long as people do something. Once you start you never know where things will go. You could prompt somebody else to think in a particular way, or think about an issue. You've no idea where that will lead.

My mum and dad met in a Young Farmers' Club dance, or more like a county show dance. I can't remember which one it was. It was basically a field and a shed and they met each other. And there was alcohol. They got married, had my sister, and then six years later had me. I grew up on a farm in west Wales. I grew up surrounded by amazing countryside but hated it because I was seeing all this cool stuff happening in all these cities across the world on the TV, and so I left when I was nineteen. I had a difficult relationship with the farm itself. Because I was really, really attached to it, but I couldn't see myself living on the farm, or at least working on the farm. So I felt really conflicted and really guilty about leaving, because it was quite a big part of my upbringing. The farm had been in our family for—I think I'm fifth generation, maybe. So it's a huge weight.

Most of my friends grew up on farms, so I never saw it as a strange thing. The only thing that made me feel like an outsider was the TV, because you never saw anything about country life, really, except for *Countryfile*. I think the TV is incredible cos it really gave me an idea of another world, and a desire to travel and to see the rest of the world and all this sort of stuff. In the winter you can't really spend much time outside, so you do end up spending a lot of time watching TV. I can look back now on the time in the countryside and think, *Oh wow*, like a rose-tinted view of it, and think it's wonderful how we had all these fields, surrounded by nature and all that, but in reality when I was a kid I just wanted to see the fireworks on New Year's, and see London and all that.

I studied theatre design. After graduating, there was no way I could afford London. So back to live in Cardiff with my sister. I started trying to do freelance theatre design in Wales, and I've been doing that for about nine years now, coming up to ten years. A friend of mine who's a director and a playwright, he was really fascinated by how I ended up in theatre, and how I ended up in London and we did a show about that. After trying to do it where we were writing a script, it just never worked, so we decided that I would just give it a go. And I did. It was terrifying. So terrifying. Toured the UK and New Zealand for that.

By the end, it stopped being terrifying, and I realised the show wasn't good anymore. There were bits of it where there was a lot of freedom to make things up and improvise a bit, around a script. And I just ran out of things to say. It felt like what we were saying in the show wasn't relevant to my life anymore, so I couldn't be genuine with it. My life became talking about my life, and the way to deal with that was to numb the real association I had with the farm. I thought that it was cathartic, the process of making it, but actually it wasn't cathartic at all, I was just finding a coping mechanism to numb those feelings. Last weekend I went back home. My parents have moved out of the farm, they're renting [it] at the moment, and I saw some other people in the house, and I just couldn't handle it. I found it really difficult.

I'm living the doorstep of my life now. Most of the time
I don't really know who I am. Because I'm very lost. And
I don't have pleasure to do things. It's hard for me. I'm
someone who don't like to show people my feeling, so I have
to act like I'm okay. I just want to be in one place and scream,
I NEED HELP. But I don't do that. I don't even have the
energy of scream. That's the problem. I don't talk to people.
I think the situation make me unsocial, because it's hard for
me to trust people.

Next year it will be three years. It's not easy. They just
need to control you. You have to go to sign every month, to
report. I don't know why they do that. And when you go to
sign, to report, you don't even know if you are coming back.
Because they can take you and put you to fly, go back. Or like
me. Once I went there, I didn't know anything, I just went to
sign. And before you get in the office you should wait hours
because there will be a long queue. Even you came early,
you have to wait. And once you get in there, before you get
into the office, there is a security check. They check you,
everything, and get a ticket number and you have to wait
again until they will call your number, your name. One day I
went there and they are like, *Oh you have a small interview.*
We need to ask you some question. They put me in a small
room and I wait like one hour, even for this interview. Nobody
was there. They took everything from me—my phone,
everything. And when they came they start asking me, *Oh*

yeah, you didn't put your fresh claim so you can't go home, you are detained now. You need to stay here. And you go to detention. I couldn't understand. They say, *Take your phone and just write down the important number in this paper and you can call the people.* What if I didn't have my charger? If my phone was dead? I don't have the number to call my solicitor, because I can't remember the name? I write the name and they took my phone again. And they tell me to wait again for two hours like this. And they put me in small room. There were a lot of asylum seekers. They gave us some crisps, but the crisps were out of date. And after that they say, *You are going to detention.* And before we go out to go to the van, they put me on the handcuffs, like a criminal. That was the worst thing in my life. I got trauma. I'm like, *I'm not a criminal, you are putting me in the van, I'm going. How can you put me?* And I start vomiting. I was crying, I was so scared. I didn't do any crime. Nothing. I just came here for help.

I don't sleep sometime. I'm scared to sleep. Because I don't wanna see things. And just I can't sleep. I saw so many blood, people killing other. So yeah, it's hard for me to sleep. I don't wanna sleep, I think—I can see blood, I can see people shout at me and it's very hard. And even sometime when I'm in the world, I feel like someone is calling me, shout at me. I have to stand and ask, and try to see like if they are really calling me. If I was there, maybe they already kill me. I don't know if I'm alive now. But I came here just for help.

63.

Even from childhood, I always had a fascination with the police. You would see them on patrol and jumping out of the helicopters—usually with the army—and checkpoints and riding along in the Land Rovers with the backs of the doors open. Which is kind of funny because back then people from a Catholic background, well, very few of them joined the police. So even though I was always fascinated by them, it never occurred to me that you could actually do it yourself.

It wasn't until I was eighteen and I moved to Belfast to go to uni. At that time there were loads of changes with the peace process and there were changes to the police service. They changed the name and recruitment to recruit more people from a Catholic background and this kind of thing. So there was all this advertising campaign going on, recruiting for the new PSNI, rather than the RUC. A television ad came on. I was sitting in the house with my friend, we were both students, and I said, *Oh I'd love to join the police*, and she said to me, *Well, why don't you then?* And then it kind of occurred to me, *Yeah, actually, there's no reason why I shouldn't.* And so I did. I never looked back.

It wasn't contentious with my family at all. My dad isn't entirely happy with it, but rather than that being for political reasons, I think it's more because of the area that he lives. He worries about me because of the security aspect. And I suppose it presents a difficulty for him, too, that I can't visit very often and have to be secretive about it. I think that's the reason for his concern rather than it really being anti-police. But the rest of my family, they wouldn't be too concerned. In fact, they were probably quite relieved because I was sixteen when I had my first daughter. So that was all a bit of an upset [laughs]. I went back to school, didn't do very well in my A levels and then moved to Belfast to repeat my A levels and discovered that in a city there was lots of partying to be done instead. Then I got a place in uni but kind of messed about at that a wee bit. And then I had my second girl—rather than graduate I had my second daughter. So yeah, they were probably just relieved that I was finally getting a proper job and maybe my life was going to get on track [laughs]. That was probably their primary concern, rather than the political climate in Northern Ireland [laughs].

I loved it. I absolutely loved it. It was brilliant. Every day is different. And all the fascinating characters that you meet. I just loved it. And I still do. I've done various roles since then. I became a detective. I would play *The Bill* as a kid, you know. We'd dress up as police and watch *Poirot* and things like that. My children laugh at me cos I love all these detective dramas. I love Agatha Christie, *Morse*, all those kinds of things. Even the real-life crime programmes—love all those. Although having some knowledge of how the police investigations really work has kind of ruined some of the dramas [laughs]. I'm going, *Oh, that's not realistic!* I always laugh—they come up with a hypothesis or they'll have put it together in their head, how they think it's happened. And of course, they're right. And they go and they confront a suspect and

94

they admit it! They always just admit it. Of course, in real life, that rarely ever happens. They'll sit there and they'll be saying, *No comment. Prove it.*

64.

They started off in Old Street in London. He was a trainee
photographer with Reuters. He met a friend from school
and he was walking down Old Street, this bloke was outside
having a fag, and they got chatting and he said, *What you
doing?* [The bloke] said, *Making jigsaws in there.* [My dad]
said, *All I'm doing is making tea at Reuters, I just wanna do
something that's a bit more worthwhile.* [The bloke] said,
Well come and make some jigsaws. I think he was getting
thirteen shillings a week [at Reuters] and he got something
like one pound and five shillings just by going to the jigsaws.
And he was very, very good at it. He masterminded the
largest jigsaw puzzle in the world at the time in 1971, which
was twenty foot eight by ten foot four, with thirty-two
thousand pieces. My parents started in '73. My dad had been
cutting jigsaws since the age of fifteen. So he'd been in it
twenty years before he set up on his own with Mum. He got
enough work in the first week for my mum to have to leave
her job. They worked together right through to the end. My
mum died in 2003 and my dad in 2016 and they both worked
in the business up until then.

I joined for temporary employment in 1979 because I
wanted to be a PE and woodwork teacher. I got my place at
Loughborough and then when I rung up to say I've got the
grades they said, *We're not doing that course anymore.* So
then I went into doing the jigsaws and I've been doing it
ever since. I always work from left to right. Nothing more

satisfying than going through that lot and it ending up on the right-hand side of your work bench, finished. Especially when you do a good job of it. When I first started I was doing piece work, so not only did you have to be skilled, but you'd got to be quick as well. But after forty-one years, I don't think about it too much now. Now I have to do the admin more and my main concern is making sure I can get the bills paid. It's keeping the factory going. Because it isn't easy. And my wife's working there and also our son's joined about six years ago. So we're a third-generation family business.

The beauty of it is, because it's unique and because it's hand-cut, it's self-correcting. When a child goes to put the pieces together, if they're not meant to go there they don't fit. With a cardboard puzzle you can get a piece to go into a slot and the pieces fit, but the picture doesn't match at all. With a wooden one you can't do that. The fret machines we use were last made in 1953. And so what we have to do is adapt them, make parts for it and keep it going. It's the same principle as a sewing machine, in our case [with a] blade rather than a needle with a thread. The blade's going up and down and you push the wood into the blade and move the wood around to create the shape. And that's why it is unique. There's no guides to go to. You just learn by experience, the craft.

Our son, he's set up a web shop. He set it all up. It's all down to him, with a friend of his. And he just told us today, I think it's been set up six months and it's turned over _____. From scratch. That's a damn good start for him. He's worked hard at it. He's done all the social media stuff, which is beyond me. And he's making it work. And I'm really pleased for him and proud of him.

I came to England and worked as an au pair for a year, because that was the way to improve and perfect my English. That's how I met him. We were both not quite reached our twenties, so quite young. When I went back to France he— well, we, obviously—thought that there was something worth having between us. In fact that summer I didn't go back to France, I went to Italy, because my parents were spending the holidays in Italy. So I joined them there. And then he sent a telegram out of the blue to say he was coming to see me in Italy. The train time at Brindisi, *I really need to see you*, whatever. And that was that.

It was quite traumatic to have to tell my parents, especially my father, that this English boy from London was coming to see me! You know—because he wanted to be with me and we wanted to be together. I'd told my sisters and brothers about it but I didn't tell my parents. So that was quite a shock. And just before he travelled to Italy he had this bike accident and he wasn't supposed to travel at all. Because he was still on very strong painkillers and he was in a lot of pain. His arm in plaster and all that—oh dear! When my father saw him I think that was a great, great shock. Because B_____ was very tall, very thin, and also he wasn't well, so he was very, very pale under his beard [laughs]. And he had sort of long, longish hair at the time, which was fashionable, you know. My dad was in complete shock [laughs]. He decided that he wasn't going to like him because he was English, and because he had a beard and because he looked like a beatnik! He was being terribly, terribly judgmental.

So that was that, really. We stayed in Italy for a bit and then he came back to Paris with us and my parents had to accommodate him where we lived. Everybody liked B____ except my dad. It's not even that he didn't like him. I think it's just that he couldn't understand, he couldn't communicate with him, so the language barrier was a terrible problem. Because B____ understood a bit of French but couldn't really converse in French. We got married about two years later. He went back to England, obviously, because he had to go back to see about his arm and to see if he could go to university and all that sort of stuff. Because when he had his very serious bike accident, that was during his A levels and he'd already applied for university, but obviously that put a stop to everything because he was in hospital for quite a few months. And then he thought, *Oh well, I'll do it later.* His plan was, before he met me, after his first accident, to go and travel the world with his bike. You know, go all over the place before he did anything else. Because he wasn't sure what direction his life was going to take, I suppose. His aim was to end up in Canada. In fact, when we married he wanted to go to Canada and I said, *There's no way I'm going to Canada, it's too far from France!* [laughs]. I just could not envisage not seeing my family for months and months. Even though my dad wasn't very happy about us being married and all that. I mean, he was happier about us being married. We didn't want to get married but B____ said, *If this is the* only way for you to leave your family then we'll just have to get married. What the hell, it doesn't matter. If you feel strong enough about it then that's what we'll do. So, yes, on it went.

My parents were quite loving to begin with, but things got a bit strange from the age of about six or seven. My dad developed an alcoholism problem, so that stunted my growth, emotional growth more than anything. There were things that I just didn't learn—how to look after my well-being. There's a lot of stuff that's missing. I think childhood trauma handicaps people quite a lot. Not that we don't all have trauma, but for me, there was a lot of things that I had to try and control when I was younger, or try and get out of. It's difficult for me to form friendships. After I did get friends, it was difficult for me to go through those channels and learn how to be a friend as well. I always thought I was a bad person.

I developed alcoholism myself. I just didn't wanna be where I was at the end of my drinking, really. I didn't want to be like that. So then I had to do something. I had to think, *Right, what do I want for myself? So stop drinking, stop smoking, and then we'll go from there.* I started doing that and then just working on, you know, forming good relationships with people, learning how to love me and other people around me, to treat people well. My dad was a single dad because my mum had to go back to Africa. So it meant that I was stunted in showing affection and love to other people. For me, when I was growing up as a teenager, putting one x, a kiss, on an end of a text to a friend was really difficult. So those are things that I had to learn. And I had to learn how to be girly as well—because I wanted to, I just didn't know how. I had to start everything later.

There's only very small instances that I would feel proud of anything that I do. There's not a lot. When they hear my story people always say, *Oh wow, you should be really proud of yourself.* I don't ever feel like that. And it's one of my things that I want to address, because in fact, I understand it. For me, looking at a friend I would say, *Be proud of yourself.* But when it comes to me, I don't think like that at all, really. I want to have good affirmations of myself, to be confident and to go out and think, *No, I can do this and be proud of what I do.* I just feel there's a lot of self-love that I need to learn.

I'm at that jumping point. I feel like I'm in that area where I can choose what I want from life. Do I want to go travelling, do I want to go back to university, do I want a family? What kind of life do I envision for myself? Because of my mental state before, I didn't have that. I couldn't see any way forward in front of me. So I didn't have a vision for life. I just went along with it. There's something more to come. I'm just not sure what it is yet. I'm not quite sure, but I'll figure it out. There'll be some sort of sign or something. It's nerve-wracking and exciting—as it would be with any stage in your life. I believe whatever happens it'll slot into place for me. So as long as I've got that belief, that I'll be okay, then I can jump off [laughs]. It's that confidence that I lack. That thing with being proud of what I've done and what I've achieved, that incorporates into that. Cos I know everybody around me can see that I can do it. But me, stuck in my body, I can't see that I can do it! So yeah, that confidence, it's been growing for a long time. So yeah.

I'll get there.

67.

I think I'm probably three weeks in now. I've just managed
to kick an adult, lifelong addiction to smoking marijuana.
I would've answered this very differently six months ago,
and with a bias towards the addiction that had a hold of me.
I'm three weeks in to I guess the most sober I've been in my
adult life. That sounds quite dramatic. I think often we think
it doesn't affect us as much as it does. And so coming out of
that now, three weeks into being sober, maybe this is a perfect
world for me? I don't know. Because I don't really know yet
who I am as an adult, without this extra layer of complexity
to who I am.

At the moment I'm very sleep-deprived, total insomnia,
can't sleep for more than maybe an hour, an hour and a half.
Crazy, crazy dreams, which people said would happen. But
now all it takes is a little bit of sunshine, nice sunny day, and
I feel euphoric. And I don't know whether that's because the
shackles have been lifted? I don't know whether it's because
I'm seeing the world differently? I don't know whether it's
connected to the fact that the sun's meant to make us feel
happy? One of my friends reckons I've had a vitamin D
shortage, but I think it's much more psychological. And when
people ask me how I feel at the moment, depending on who's
asking me I tend to say either that my inner six-year-old is
now my outer self, or that I feel like a six-year-old on LSD.
Mild LSD, though! My emotional sensor is somewhat off
and a bit wobbly. I do have these moments of non-euphoria

balancing the euphoria. I'm not gonna go as far as to say depression, cos I think whilst I was smoking I experienced more severe depression than I have since.

I mean, added to this, at the beginning of the year—it's a really long, complicated story that is not relevant really—but I swapped my diet. I gave up refined sugar as part of that. Within these last three weeks I gave up everything, basically. Everything that's a drug. So tea, caffeine, nicotine, obviously ganja. It's not like I particularly did any other drugs—I mean, I did when I was younger—but everything is gone now and so the world is a whole new place to me that I'm really looking forward to discovering! I'm just sort of embracing the world as it is.

A friend of mine scared me a little bit. He said it was seven years after he gave up smoking before he got a good night's sleep. But he's also been addicted to sleeping pills in the meantime. I can kind of see why. I had actually gone to the doctor's. For the first time I let the medical profession know—I really hope she didn't write it down—that I was smoking and that I'd stopped smoking. I was genuinely worried that sleep psychosis might set in before I got a good night's sleep. And you know, she wrote down two medications on a piece of paper and I said, *I'm gonna stop you there cos I'm not gonna do that. I'm not gonna go down a medicated route to fix this.* She insisted on describing it to me anyway, and one of them she said, *These are really, really addictive, but don't worry cos I'll only prescribe them to you the once.* And I was like, *You don't get it, do you?*

If they're that addictive I'll find them. I'll find something that fills that hole.

I still long for a really good night's sleep—just to be asleep for more than two hours and to not have my dreams interrupting. But at the moment that's a goal for me, that's something that I'm looking forward to happening—whether it happens in a month, whether it happens in a year. I pray it happens sooner than seven years!

68

I was in an annex and then they moved me into the main building. There was a girl that sat next to me and we became really, really good friends. We used to go to lunch together every day. Then we started to go jogging together. I'm not really a friends-at-work person. When I was younger—and I think especially coming from a Caribbean family—there were certain things that were alien to me. Things like going to the pub after work was not, culturally, something that we did. But anyway, the story is this girl. We used to go jogging. After work, twice a week, we'd jog from the office in the City to Canary Wharf and back, which was 10K, six miles. And then maybe once a month we'd go for a curry after. Or sometimes we'd have a drink after work. One of these particular days we did our usual thing of going for a run, came back, we went to have a curry. And we had quite a lot to drink. By the time I got home I was quite bladdered, put it that way. It was a Friday after work. And when I got home, thinking about my friend, I wrote this song. I remember thinking, *The song's come to my head, I've got to get it down.* And I got a scrap of paper and wrote the whole song. And it took me another couple of years, but eventually I recorded it and she was able to hear it. That song always reminds me of her.

I loved that job—a lot. It's a job that gave me an income for the first time, that gave me an income that I could manage my life on, where I wasn't struggling. She used to always say to me, *You're my hero*. Because, I dunno, because I had a grandchild, I worked, I had a band, I did all these things. And we just got on so well. We're still friends, but the closeness of the relationship stopped, which is a shame. We kind of fell out because I went through a lot of workplace racism in the end in that job. And nobody there understood. You care about people and you think that they care about you, but they just don't understand. It's like if I said to you what it's like to be a single mother, you wouldn't understand. You'd empathise, but you might not understand. She just didn't have a concept of it. A lot of things when you're being racially targeted in the workplace, a lot of the things are covert, so it's not that people always see what goes on. But when people make excuses for the people that are doing hard, horrible things to you, that's when I started to withdraw a bit—because I thought we were really good friends. And now I'm being really, really treated badly in this place and you're making excuses for the people that are treating me badly.

This manager made my life an absolute misery. He was racist. He was sexist. He micromanaged me. It was three years of hell. I ended up having to go off work for six months and for six months I literally just lied on a sofa and went on YouTube. I couldn't do anything. It was so debilitating and it was so difficult to cope with. And it affected me so much. Affected me so badly. And that's why I sometimes get the impression that people think I'm a bit out there and a bit edgy, but they don't understand some of the things I've had to go through. She started going out for drinks with them!

And then obviously I ended up leaving the workplace with a settlement. I don't really speak to her anymore. I'm more on the odd Facebook thing. I know she got married about a year ago. But yeah, you inspired me. I'm going to get in contact with her. This story's not about the racism, it's about the girl I wrote the song [for].

69.

Somebody wait for us in airport. They took us to some
house. A lot of people there. And that night was almost a
fight—guns, you know. I was in a mess and I come here—still
a mess! This is worse. We stayed three days, living in the
room like five, six people. Then the guy, he came, he said,
Tomorrow evening, get ready.

In the afternoon we come up from hotel—*Inside! Inside!*
I think we went inside more than eight people in the car!
The driver was really, really fast. And we went to the border.
A van was waiting there. We don't know where we're going.
Just I remember this guy, he was catching people from
the car and he threw them in the van. And the van again,
driving fast. Your heart's going *bam bam bam*. Sometimes
you're laughing, sometimes you're crying. We don't know
where we are. It's like mountain border, border between
Turkey and Greece. It was a little bit hell. We stay two days
there. Cold, no food, no water, shouting. If you argue with
them, they take you somewhere so we cannot see. I dunno
what they was doing, but I noticed that if someone complain
he go there and he come back, he's quiet. I dunno what
magic they have!

And then we cross the river. Like a small boat. Before we
get into the end of the river, Turkish army, they came. They
shooting with I think it's plastic. Just you hear *BAM*. When
we hear, people jumping. There is a lady and child. So we
helped her to get out. Cos there was water and river, it got

power. We passed the river, walking, walking, walking, and then we found small city. We found some fountain, we wash, we clean, we went into the bus stop. The police came. They took us. We stayed there twenty-three days. And where we stayed, in the room, was like four people, I don't remember where from. They got problem with the police so they make fire in the ceiling. We almost died, [more] than sixty [of us]. Because it's burnt and no windows. The police came and opened the doors—*Get out! Get out!*

From there we went to Athens. Athens was worse! No language, no money, how can you survive? There is some charities there, they give us food, some pasta. You eat pasta, you go to sleep straight away. They putting something in pasta, some medicine to sleep I think. Because at park, they delivering the food, you finish pasta, you slept straight away. I was thinking, *I get out from hell but I came to hell, exactly the same.* Different country, different language, no money. No phone, no contacts, no friends.

Some guys, they said, *If you want we take you to other city. There is a port there and the ship, they go to Italy.* There is some Afghanis, they put you in a van, close, if you die, you die. How you say in Arabic? If you die, you die, if you don't die, *salaam alaikum* [laughs]. So. People, they put you in the van and they close the van. If you get out in Italy alive, congratulations! Not vans, it's a lorry. I remember my friend, he was in coffin. Where you put dead people. Those people, they put a lot inside, inside the coffins. I don't know. God. I don't know. They don't care.

I went to Napoli. I found some charity there. Like, you sleep one week, food, shower, everything. I stayed there one week. And I come to French. I found some people there in French that are related to the group I was in in _____. And I say, *What the fuck? What can I do now?* And say, *I'm going to Belgium.* From Belgium I dunno, to be honest. I found myself in England. Ten years. And in England, the same thing. No language, no friend, no money. Sleep in a park, sleep in some cars, sleep in some squats. Four years street homeless. And I start thinking maybe that is my life, that is the end.

70.

I was brought up on a diet of all things American. That comes partly from the place I grew up in, Munich, where there were a lot of American soldiers stationed. There was a part in Munich that looked just like an American suburb. That's where all the soldiers lived, and they had their own JCPenney, for example, and their own high school, and they had the broad streets with those front gardens with a driveway up to the house, and it looked 100 per cent like in America. It was crazy. They had fairs and stuff, including inviting the Germans, and it felt just like being in Midwestern USA somewhere.

So there was that, but then also my parents were really, really into Afro-American culture. They were really into free jazz and they invited musicians over and they worked with an artist who they then supported as well. They got him over and his wife and his son came over as well, and they lived in the flat opposite us on the hallway, and we became very good friends. We were maybe eight, nine? A really big part of all this is when the mum made spare ribs for us, the way they do it. I was always a meat eater, and my family always enjoyed meat, and they made the spare ribs, and I still make those exact same spare ribs with that secret sauce. I'm completely obsessed by it [laughs]. I just couldn't believe how much fun it was to eat that stuff, and how tasty it was.

That's how I fell in love with anything American. Michael Jackson, Lionel Richie and Diana Ross and all that. But also watching stuff like *Unknown Stuntman* and *Knight Rider*.

That just created this total utopia. Even with all its faults, even with the racial problems and everything, it just created this total utopia in my head. When I was nineteen I went to New York, and it was like all my dreams come true. I walked around and I couldn't believe it. I could have stood on the street corner all day, just watched the world. And then I came back and, you know, life happened—there was no agency to earn money or the kind of foresight to actually pack up my stuff and go there because my life was in Munich. And so I started to study and go to Hamburg, and then Berlin, and then friends of mine moved to London and I came to London. The first time I came to Dalston, where I live now, I went down Kingsland Road and I just got the exact same buzz I got when I walked through New York. It was just completely loose, everyone was doing their thing—the barrel barbecues in the side streets and music everywhere, it was just chaos, but in the best way. So I thought, *Let's try that out first and see how it goes*, and then I met _____ and then we stayed here.

And now all of that, a lifetime of believing in that, in the last three, four years, it all came tumbling down. I mean, it was a really slow-motion tumble [laughs]. It was like, *Oh, that bit moved a bit. Oh, and that bit moves a bit too, I wonder where that's going? Oh, that's knocking on this one, oh, okay, and this one is touching that one, okay.* That's how it felt. Watching it in slow motion but knowing the direction it's gonna go, but not believing that it would actually really disintegrate like that. It's something that you lived with and you always go to for comfort. America is such an insanely complex construct, and it's also a placeholder for so many things. You can put in there whatever you want. That's exactly what's going on there right now—everyone interprets it differently. I'm still in love with American culture, 100 per cent. I'm still invested in it and follow it closely. But there's a definite fracture now. Having that taken away at first felt really scary, then all of a sudden it felt weirdly liberating. I don't have to go there anymore. I can find something else.

71.

I get a lot of panic attacks. Not a lot, I've had a few. I think
the first one I actually ended up in an ambulance cos you
don't know what they are, and they're intensely physical.
Your whole body will freeze, and your hands go into claw
hands, which are pretty strange. It's like hypertension, or
something. The whole surface of your skin, all over your
body, your epidermis just tingles. And I think it only happens
in the moment of forgetting what a panic attack is. You think,
*Oh no, this time it's really different. Why is no one taking it
seriously, because I am dying?* And then someone tells you to
look at them and breathe a few times normally and it's over,
like that. But yeah, it's more bodily than anything else.

The weird thing is I've had them a few times around my
best friend. We do long walks together. We'll do the Camino
de Santiago or the West Highland Way, and it's happened
on those long walks. The first time it was in a town in Rioja
in Spain. There was a festival on. We were walking in the
autumn, there were these series of local town festivals
happening, and we ended up passing through quite a lot
of them, cos they have them on different days. We were
watching a huge procession down the street where people
were carrying these twenty-foot papier mâché kings and
queens. I was looking at them and I had this moment of
intense joy. And then it span very quickly backwards into this
panic attack. Once, I ended up being hospitalised for a broken
wrist and I did so much laughing gas that I had one. My

friend has a theory that it's joy. I don't, I try not to, I don't really agree. But I think there is something about moments when the body is overwhelmed, or overwhelming moments.

I think I am a bit afraid of that. Once your body knows the route somewhere, it will just go there, if that makes sense. I think I'm afraid of that happening—in drug use, or drinking too much. But then again the fear must have both pre-dated and caused the panic attack [laughs], which is quite weird. I guess it's about loss of control, maybe? Or something that should go down the route to joy—that energy accidentally goes somewhere else, or down the wrong path? I mean, loss of control, being overwhelmed, that euphoria? I don't know. I think it's probably just like a really simple, basic fear of death. People often say the moment before you die, you do feel an intense joy, euphoria. I literally become unconnected. An endorphin rush and a fear of death. I can't remember which book, but Milan Kundera says vertigo's not the fear of falling, it's the fear that you really want to fall. And the horror comes from recognising that desire in yourself. So though fear seems maybe at first like it's the desire to put as much distance as possible between you and whatever that thing is, it could also be, *I want this but what would happen then?*

I worry about getting them in the kind of normal situations when someone would worry about getting them—the cinema, the theatre, any kind of public event, a party, somewhere where you have to sit down and you don't know if you can sneak out, that kind of thing. But it never happens then, maybe because I'm hyper-aware that it might happen.

But then I think the whole point of doing the walks is getting outside your day-to-day life, and also you are under more physical strain than normal. And I don't know—this is the whole desire/fear thing again—maybe one of the reasons to do the walk is a desire to break out of something. I'm not spiritual at all, but the pilgrimage as a route to knowledge, or as a route towards *something else*. When you think about the people who did it, the pilgrims probably hoped [for] epiphanies, moments of the body breaking down, so maybe it's the kind of space where that would happen. I mean, I don't know why she still walks with me [laughs].

72.

The other day I swallowed a nail by accident. About two centimetres long. I was pinning a shelf up, and the old classic, you know—you need both hands, just put the nail in the mouth. I actually don't know how it slipped, cos I had a very, very firm grip on it, in my mouth, and then suddenly it's gone. Have you ever had it where you swallow gum and there's that split second where it's here and you think, *I can catch it, I can stop it*, and then it's gone? It was like that. So that's how it came about. I was very calm about the whole thing. Because—I mean, this gives me a very bad rep for putting things in my mouth—but I once had a sewing needle stuck in my mouth, at the back. And that was much scarier. It was kind of trapped. And sewing needles are thin, and that wouldn't just cushion itself nicely inside of me, it would just go straight through or something. I didn't swallow that, I managed to fish that out, but this time round, I was much calmer.

It got stuck in my throat for about half an hour and then it was just there and I could feel it and almost push it a little bit, and I was thinking, *What position is it like inside of there? What's it doing? Is it close to piercing something? Is it gonna go somewhere?* I called the doctor and they asked me to swallow some water, and I really didn't want to because I thought, *Well, if it's here, maybe they can get it out somehow?* And the idea of ingesting a nail is a lot scarier than having it somewhere where I know where it is. And then I swallowed and it went a bit down here, and I was like, *Which way up is it?* And I kind of imagined it travelling. I was wishing that there was a camera on the end of it. And then the woman said to me, *You just have to wait until it goes through your system.* As I was going to bed in the evening I thought, *I could be internally bleeding right now and I wouldn't know.* And I was wondering what it looks like inside and whether it's going all around, whether it was just stuck to its little canal and fed through? Was it swimming? I kind of imagined it getting a little bit cushioned into the side of me for a bit, and then getting a bit dislodged. They say your small intestine is god knows how long, so what is it like inside there? I imagine it being this really sensory place where it's really weird, like gushing noises and [glugging noises] and all that, and this little nail having a bit of a swim along the canal, and doing its own little thing.

At points when it was touching a bit inside, I was thinking, *Oh goodness no, this is not a nice image.* I'm thinking [splatting noise], like straight puncture. But then I quite like the idea of this little nail having a nice journey on the inside of me. I like the idea that it goes in me and will have this whole journey that I will never ever see or know, and will come back out most likely exactly the same as it went in. It's not gonna be affected by anything in me. I fantasised about the idea of fishing it out and saving it, cos it's like, *You've been through me.* Everything else, we eat it and it's a bit gruesome but it comes out a completely different form. I don't know why, I really became quite connected to this nail.

It's like it was my nail, almost. Still is my nail. It's my thing, even though it's quite dangerous. Now I'm a bit like, *Hmm, maybe I don't want it to leave me, maybe I want this foreign object inside me, just swimming around forever, doing its own little thing.* I think that would be quite nice. Yeah, it would be very nice. It would be amazing if it had somehow changed shape whilst it was inside of me, but I don't think that could happen.

73.

I'm different things in different circumstances, with different people. I have my personal personality if you like, the one that I am when I'm alone in the house. I have my husband personality. I have my father personality. I have my professional personality, I have the personality that I am when I'm around friends. And all of those, I think, overlap to a greater or lesser extent. What I'm seeing in my mind now is some kind of Venn diagram, some multifaceted Venn diagram of these different personalities. I think what I'm saying here doesn't necessarily just relate to me. It relates to everybody. What we're like when we're with our parents or what we're like when we're with the mayor or what we're like when we're with the lads from uni or people you grew up with. All those personalities, I think, are slightly different. And I think some of them are more removed than others. In an ideal world my view is that those personalities wouldn't differ too much. And I think that would be the sign of a genuine and honest person. Do my personalities differ, though? Yeah, they do. They do. I'm a different person when I'm out with the lads watching football than I am when I'm with my two daughters. Language is an obvious difference there, particularly at the football!

Our time in those spaces is really valuable to us. You know, I use the example of what I'm like when I go to the football. I actually go to the football with my nephew and my eighty-three-year-old dad. So those spaces, again, are overlapping. I'm not going down the football, drinking a load of pints, being lairy and singing obnoxiously rude songs at the opposition fans. I'm going down there to spend time with my dad. And my nephew. I say my nephew, he's in his early thirties now. So it's my dad, his son and his grandson. We really value spending time with him and he loves spending time with us. And it's a lovely thing to do and it's a lovely juxtaposition of those two personality spaces. To see my dad calling the referee a wanker! It's quite amusing because my dad is of that generation whereby he didn't swear in front of the wife or the children. I know for a fact that he would've swore in his personality space with his mates. But the first time you see it, you're like, *Ooh, that's strange. You alright there, Dad? Getting a bit carried away are we?*

Well, he is. He is one, isn't he?

And you can kind of jump back out of that space and back into the Dad space again.

I think that's what we're all like as people, not just as adults, but as people. We all have our own spaces and the context determines which personality space we're in. I think that there are some people who you see whose personality spaces in different contexts are so widely diverse, it can make people feel a bit uncomfortable. But there are also some people who are just that one personality through all contexts, and I think that's a little bit uncomfortable.

Who am I? I'm that one person with different hats on and over time some of the hats fall off, I guess. You know, as you shed your acquaintances or as people who you love pass away. I'm a different son to my dad than I was to my mum. My mum passed away a couple years ago. We had a great relationship. We were very fortunate. But I've got a great relationship with my dad as well. And I'd even go as far to say I've got a better relationship now with my dad than I did when my mum was alive. I think that that relationship of me and my mum, or my mum to me, dominated the relationship of my dad and I. And now that that's no longer the case we're able to be a little bit more like the true us. To each other. I would get Mum back at the drop of a hat if I could do. I don't think it was a negative thing. It's just that relationship's been given the time to grow. And I value that now. That's one of the things that comforts me—knowing that Mum's gone but I still got Dad.

74.

I'm having a very difficult time at the moment, so.

I find myself in a situation where I'm homeschooling my son, not because his school hasn't gone back but because he's recently been diagnosed with a lot of special educational needs. It was weird timing because the school told me that he had special educational needs at a parents' evening, and then literally the Monday after that we went into lockdown. There was timing issues there, but I suppose I was just a bit concerned that I've had him at school all that time, same school for four years, and I had literally no idea about this. I'd been to quite a lot of parents' evenings at that school, I knew the teachers. In the early parents' evenings I might have gone in with a little list of notes on my phone about things I wanted to talk about, but this one I had a couple of things in my head but I wasn't prepared for it. I dashed in, rushing from somewhere, and sat down, and then . . . You know when people drop a bombshell on you and you try and stay composed and listen to what they're saying, but you can't really hear the rest of it, can you? You just go into a little mini-shock. I was just so surprised. I was just so, so surprised.

If he'd carried on at school, I suppose I'd have called in the next week and said, *You could've told me in a better way than that.* I would've had it out a bit and then we would've carried on and it probably wouldn't have been such a big spike, it would have been a bit of a wobble. But because of the timing, it meant that it was that and then nothing. Just nothing. And of course all the services were shut. I had to do the psychology thing myself, cos there was no government things available. I had to do a private thing. Even now, getting appointments with the CAMHS, the Childhood and Adolescent Mental Health Services, it's months and months and months and months of waiting cos everything's backlogged. And so here I am, trying to work and homeschooling him. I'm trying to create an entire educational programme for him, without a school, while working full-time, and it's really hard. But it's also really interesting, in lots of ways, and it's terrifying, and it's a huge amount of responsibility—working out what are these things that are going on with his brain?

I suppose part of it is that I did suddenly feel like, *Hold on a minute, I think you should at least know a bit about what's going on in your kid's brain!* I'd obviously handed it all over and just thought, *Ah, he'll be alright.* And then it turns out that he really wasn't alright, and I had no idea. So I suppose this is me thinking, *Let's see what's going on here, at least try and understand what's going on, and spend more time with him and see what's out there and do all this stuff with him.* And then I'll send him back to school once I know what the hell's going on so that I can start to address it.

It's nice to get out of that feeling, especially in September, especially with going back to school, [where] you feel like you're getting back on a treadmill, you're doing things in the way that things are done, and you're trapped in it. There's a comfort to it, but you're also trapped in a cycle. For me, I've always railed against that, I've never done the things

127

you're supposed to do, and for me it's quite nice to feel like we're exploring a different way of doing something and trying something that is unconventional, and making it up ourselves. As stressful as it is, it is also exciting.

I was just thinking in the bath this morning about how this has happened, really. I'm a single parent. I got pregnant eight years ago and I didn't stay with his dad. And it's funny, isn't it, cos here I am, eight years later with this big boy and now, at eight, you start to see what a person really is, who was in there all that time. You think when you're having a baby that you're having a baby. Of course you're not. You're having a whole person, and you're having their whole life. And you've got no idea what that means.

75

I was one of seven kids and we were proper poor. We never went on holidays or anything like that. A holiday was just not a thing. It was never even considered. I'm sure my parents maybe dreamt about it, but it was never gonna happen. We were on welfare a lot. And, you know, my mum and dad, they were like chalk and cheese, should never [have] been together. So it was quite a volatile household. There was no money. It was quite hellish sometimes. But with seven kids, you know, you have a good time with your brothers and sisters. You've got nothing and you become very creative within that. But my mum was doing all the running—going to get the information to get us free dinners or to get us vouchers for school uniform. She got savvy and I guess she was learning all the ways to get freebies out of the government. Because it's there. It's for you. When you're poor you're even more proud. It's like, *I'm not gonna do that.* You go as far as you can trying to do it all. And you can't. One day you concede—*I'm defeated.*

So anyway, with all this searching for what is available for us, she found out from the welfare that they would send us away on this little holiday. And we went to Maidstone in Kent, right? [Laughs] And it was like, *Oh my god, we're going on a holiday!* We've never been away so nobody's got a suitcase or anything. You'd pack your stuff in whatever bag you've got. My mum comes with us. We stay in this guesthouse and it's by the sea. And I've never been by the sea before at that point. You can imagine—we're in Maidstone in Kent, we're the only Blacks around, so you go out and it's weird cos people are looking at you. There's no love. But, you know, we don't care. We're gonna have a good time.

It was run by this husband and wife. She was asthmatic and he was weird—he was just weird. All of us brothers and sisters were all in one room at the top. We wake up in the morning and we go nuts—we're jumping from bed to bed, we're just having the maddest time. I remember one morning, [there's] banging on the door. We freeze: *Who's that?!* And then we have to delegate who's gonna open the door. And it was probably me cos I was always delegated to face the adults. So I'd open the door and it's the woman, the wife. And she's like [long wheezing sounds], *Stop.* She's asthmatic, right? So she's telling us off but panting, so she could only get one word out in between all the panting [laughs]. *Stop* [pants] *jumping* [pants]. And we're dying! She tells us off, we gotta listen—it seems like an eternity that this woman is telling us off cos she can't get all her words out cos she's out of breath coming up all the stairs to the top of the house. We were like, *Yeah, we're really sorry. We're really sorry.* She shut the door. Well, I mean, eruption! We go nuts again and she's waiting outside the door. So she goes, *I'm not joking!*

And then we'd go down for breakfast. The husband would put the plates down with whatever you were having for breakfast that day. And with each plate that he put down he'd go, *Er-huh* [groan]. *Er-huh.* And we were like, *What's happening?* He'd do it with every single plate. We thought, *Is he doing it just for us?* But no, he'd go to the other tables and it would be like, *Er-huh*, so that was a source of hilarity as well. We had a crazy-arse asthmatic woman and this nutter. Then you had this old guy. He would take his dentures out and he'd file them.

I remember this time as, on one hand, really sad, you know, because obviously, looking back, I know we were there because we were really skint and we were charity cases. But on the other hand, we had this time together, me and my brothers and sisters, being out in this weird place, and it's left a proper good memory. It's more the characters and the house I remember, not so much the going to the beach. But yeah, it was like, *We've been on holiday!* You tell your white friends and they just go, *Yeah, alright. We go to Spain.* You was kind of ridiculed a bit, but to us it was wild.

76.

I haven't talked to my mother for the past twenty years.
I haven't seen her for the past twenty years. My mother
used to suffer from obsessive-compulsive disorder, among
other problems, and I suppose that is still the case. Since I
remember until I left my parents' home when I was eighteen
years old, my mother was always washing things—washing
her hands, washing everything—and she asked my sister and
myself to be witnesses of how she washed everything. How
she was washing the washing machine for doing the laundry
after using it, how she washed her hands, even watch when
she was having a shower so that we could remind her that
she was clean. She was afraid of everything and she thought
that she would get infected by [hesitates] the world, really.

It was very hard to grow up like that. I sort of rebelled
against having to watch her washing things, and she would
get very angry. I didn't stop seeing my mother because of
the obsessive-compulsive disorder. I pitied her for that and I
always felt a kind of compassion for her anguish about being
infected by the world—it was obviously very, very profound.
But she was a very violent woman—physically violent, but
mostly emotionally violent. A very cruel woman. And that's
why I haven't been in touch with her for so long. I try not
to think of her very much because I find it disturbing and
painful, but since I've been in the lockdown for three weeks
now, because I'm supposed to be one of the vulnerable ones
according to my GP, I've been thinking of her. I thought

I had managed to save myself from my mother's fears, in many ways, and I've never been afraid of being infected by anything, really. But now I am. As is everybody else in the world, I think. So I've been washing my hands a lot and cleaning everything, absolutely everything. I am doing my shopping online because my GP doesn't want me to go to shops, and everything that arrives in the house I've been cleaning, wiping with disinfectant wipes, and washing it when it's washable, and washing my hands over and over again and having strange thoughts: *How do I wash the thing I wash the things with?* Fearing that everything may contain this tiny little thing that is terrifying us all.

And I've been thinking of my mother, I've been thinking how on earth may she be coping with this? My sister, who I haven't seen for twenty years either, *inherited*, so to speak, the obsessive-compulsive disorder, and I felt anguish about them, thinking how terrified they must be. I can't imagine how things may be going for them. I've felt a lot of compassion for them. I can say now that I understand the feeling that my mother had to struggle with on her own for so long. On her own because even if we watched her washing everything, the suffering was hers. We just couldn't understand it. The suffering it caused us was of a different kind. I understand her fear now. But I'm also being very careful about not becoming an obsessive-compulsive person myself, so I've been wondering how much can I really wash my hands? How much is it healthy to wash my hands? My hands—I can't recognise them now, they are really raw. I think many people have the same problem. Even if I use hand cream they look horrible. I've been comparing notes with friends—*How much is it healthy to wash things?*

This is the secret I want to share, that the pandemic has made me think about my mother and my sister. Not so much about whether they are catching the virus or not. In that sense I am concerned about absolutely everybody I know and everybody I don't know. I am concerned about their fear and I am trying to do everything in my power not to get infected by *fear*, as much as it's possible. It's a strange, detached way to think of one's mother. I know I'm not going to look for her to ask her how she is. And I know she won't look for me either. I don't think she wishes I am well. She never has. She has always wished me to be [hesitates] dead, I suppose. But I wish she is okay, and I wish so much that the pandemic has not exacerbated her utter fear of being infected by the world. I, luckily enough, think that the world is, despite everything, beautiful. And I am determined not to fear the world.

77

I remember in W_____, all the woman wanted was a joint off us. It's not very big, W_____, she was saying, so everyone knows everyone's business. She was a teacher so she was like, *I can't get weed or anything.* She dropped a hint: *Ooh, that smells nice.* I just went, *Do you want some? Come and have a joint with us.* She went, *No, no, you're alright. Can you sort us one out?* And I just gave her one. It's no skin off our backs, is it? If she's on it, it's better for us. Then we don't have to creep around, do we?

Where we're from everyone smokes weed. There's no one who doesn't smoke weed. It's part of life, isn't it? So we're not really that bothered. But some people proper turn their noses up against it. And you've got to be careful, haven't you? They don't like it. Cos they don't really know much about it, I suppose. I'd rather be in a room full of people stoned than a room full of people drunk. I was going up football with all my mates and we were going, *Yeah, it'll be good if we have a tear-up.* Then I had a joint and I was like, *I hope nothing happens now. I just want to sit here and watch the football.* And everyone was just chilled out.

I was just in Spain and it's sort of half-legal over there. It's a bit sketchy. Because it's legal in Catalonia—Barcelona and all that and along the way. But then on the other side of it, it's not legal. My mate is living there and he said he's got to be very careful travelling with it. When you're in there you can have it but when you're leaving, don't get caught.

Because on the motorway you're going down the road and you'll come across these random drugs checkpoints.

America, you have to have a card, you know what I mean? You apply, you get a licence, then you can go and buy it. My mate just did Camp America. Me best mate. Not last year, the year before. And he's saying—he's in California—you can just buy a card. It's not even like you have to be a national. He just bought one. On the front of the beach they'll just sign you up. They'll take you in the shop and they'll say, *You've got chronic back pain*. Then you can buy weed wherever you want in America. New York as well. It's legal in New York. He says imagine if you're in upstate New York, walking down the thing, and you just see like a big weed picture and you just go in and buy it. Brilliant.

Everyone's smoked weed, haven't they? Everyone. Everyone's had a try of it. You've got to look at Amsterdam, yeah? The rate of people who take harder drugs, like heroin and cocaine, is lower. Because they've got the opportunity of going and sitting in the coffee shops and getting stoned. They've got safe places for the heroin addicts. So instead of having them on the streets and that, if they want to go and take heroin then they go to a massive place run by the government and they get clean needles and that and shoot up in there. Keep them off the street, innit? Which is a good thing because I don't know what it's like in the centre of London but you go through the centre of Manchester, mate, and it's [whistles]. That Spice is summat else, it's just amazing. Every ten metres there's someone there, sat on

136

the street begging, out their minds. People are dying off it. People die off it on a daily basis. It's fish food isn't it, or plant fertiliser? It's madness. And it's highly addictive. You ought to see the state of people. You get groups of them, they're all like zombies. It's all around town, I'm telling you.

I was in Manchester city centre last week and I saw them arresting people for begging. You could tell the two guys that they got were genuinely homeless. They didn't look like they were on drugs, they didn't look drunk or anything like that, do you know what I mean? And they were literally pulled up and arrested for begging. Me and my mate were wondering what was going on, so we was like, *What are you arresting them for? Leave them alone. What have they done?* And they go, *They're begging. It's against the law now.* And I was like, *Wow. You got nowhere to go and you're sat on the street and you can't even beg?*

78

I went back home last month to see my folks. They're people
who have a fucking television on in every single room, and
no one's in it. It does my nut in! I walked into one of the
rooms where the television was on and no one was in there—
there was that Barnardo's ad, and it just made me think, *Fuck,
that's pretty much exactly what happened to me.* What this
girl was talking to this therapist about. *We started off just
messaging,* she says. The equivalent of that in those days was
he used to write me notes whilst we were at work, during
the quiet moments. *I was fourteen,* she says. I was 'of age' at
sixteen but still a virgin. *I can't believe he liked me,* she says.
I guess I must've felt the same. He was a man and I was a
teenage girl, after all. *He was always buying me things,* she
says. He did the same for me. *Gave me lifts from school,* she
says. He used to drive me home after work and if I called him
he would come and get me and take me anywhere I wanted to
go. *We started to go back to his,* she says. He wanted to show
me where he lived and I wanted to see. *He asked me to do
stuff. He said it was normal because he loved me,* she says.
He didn't move as fast with me. First, he told me he loved
me and said that I probably didn't want to lose my virginity
to someone my own age, as they wouldn't know what to do.
That I probably wanted to lose my virginity to someone with
a bit of experience. I was sixteen, he was thirty-two.

When I was thirteen I used to work in a supermarket.
I was working in a supermarket illegally cos I wanted to

earn some money. This guy used to come in every Sunday and I would be on the till in the supermarket and he would always say hello. I recognised him from this shop that I used to go in, which was a bit of a cult shop, a surf shop where everyone used to hang out. I can't really remember how I ended up getting a job there. It might have been that he asked if I wanted a job there? I really don't know. Anyway, I did want a job there, I got the job there and I was working Saturdays and in the holidays. Throughout the winter it's pretty quiet in that shop, so we would just hang out and talk and stuff. You get close to people when you're in those kind of situations. I can't really remember when he admitted to me how he felt about me. But I was probably only about fourteen or fifteen, maybe? At the time, you think you're really mature and you know exactly what's going on and all of that. It's only in recent years that I've thought that [that] age difference is fucking shocking, really [laughs]. Because I was still a child. I mean, I've looked at photos again and thought, *Yeah, actually I do look like a woman.* But he knew how old I was. He had a girlfriend, she was at uni. I think she must've been about sixteen when they got together. So there was a big age difference between them. But obviously not as much as me. So while she was at university I would hang out with him. I think he was just quite lonely, actually. He lived with someone else who was never there. His girlfriend was away. He didn't have loads of friends. It didn't bother me that he had a girlfriend. I believed that he loved me. I don't know if I loved him. I think I just said it because I thought I was supposed to. What else do you say when someone tells you that? When a thirty-two-year-old man who's your manager tells you that?

I'd kind of really like to have a conversation with him about it now, just to see what he's got to say for himself about it, but I can't, because he's dead. He died of a heroin overdose. I know so many heroin addicts over there. It kind of flooded the island. And I don't really know why. I think there was a really bad batch that came into the island because the week that he died, a few other people died as well. So fuck knows what was mixed in with it. He died in his kitchen. It was a really grim end for him. And he was only, he must've been thirty-eight, I think. Which is really fucking young. And at that time I thought, *Oh, that's quite old* [laughs]. Cos you do when you're a kid, don't you?

79.

I studied different religions—Hinduism, Sikhism, New Age, Mormon, Jehovah Witness, Christianity, Islam—and, in the end, I started saying, *There is no God.* I had knowledge, but I don't have any relationship with Jesus.

I met with one Christian friend and he tried to evangelise me. He said that *You can see your God.*

I said, *Oh, if I can see him then he's not God, he's something I can see and I can observe.*

But every time he kept saying that: *You can see your God, you can see your God.*

And one day I challenged him and I said, *Okay, I want to see your God.* And I asked him, *What do you need to do?*

He said, *You don't need to do anything. Before you go to bed just pray a short, simple prayer and my Jesus will come.*

I said, *Okay. I have done so many funny things, crazy things, so let's do this thing as well.*

So he taught me this prayer: CREATOR OF THIS UNIVERSE, OUR TRUE LIVING GOD, WHOEVER YOU ARE, COME! I WANT TO SEE YOU. That's it. He didn't mention Jesus, he didn't mention Allah, he didn't mention Krishna, or Buddha, anything. And I was impressed by this. And I don't know why, I challenged him and I said, *Okay, your God has thirty days. I want to see him within thirty days.*

I prayed for twenty-nine nights and nobody came. Every day I used to tell him, *See, there is no God.* And every time he used to tell me, *No, there is one God.* And still there are ten days, there are five days, there are three days. His faith was very strong. Thirtieth night, when I was sleeping in my bedroom, I heard a voice from outside which called me. I rushed to the kitchen door and looked outside. Nobody was there. And I moved back—because I was scared. And after some time I hear that same voice again, which called me. I rushed to the kitchen door and looked outside. Nobody was there.

And then I saw a man in white clothes. He came on the terrace and from terrace he walked down. And he came and he stood just right in front of my face. And he asked me, *Will you not allow me to come into your bedroom?* I was completely frozen. I couldn't say even one single word. I moved back and I sit on my bed. And he follow me and sit to the feet side. And he said he is Jesus. I didn't believe him. I said, *Okay, if you are Jesus then my brother and my sister-in-law, they are sleeping in that bedroom. Go and bring them here.* So he went, he called them, they came and they sit to the other side of the bed. And we all four of us prayed together. And after prayer my brother and my sister-in-law went back to their room. I had so many questions which I wanted to ask from this man, so I asked all my questions and he answered all my questions. And then this man left.

Next day, early in the morning, my sister-in-law came to my room and she asked me, did I watch a nightmare last night? I said, *No!* She said that she and her husband, they came in my room, they saw me, I was praying and I was crying. And then I asked her, *Did you see somebody else in my room?* They said, *No, you was alone.* And then I asked them, *Did you pray with me?* They said, *No.* And then I testified to them, and I told them Jesus visited me, and I told them whole story what happened and this is their words, they said, she and her husband, they could feel the presence of God in my room. And that was the day, 30 September 1994, when God changed my life, completely, dramatically. And that's why I know that our God is real. He's so, so real! And we don't need just head knowledge, we need to have a relationship with him. And I tell this thing to every single person I meet. So if you don't know Jesus until now, ask him and he will come and he will talk to you. And he will take away all your doubts, all your confusions, because he's so real. He's not a fancy thing, he's real. He's a real God. He's real. And he's same yesterday, today and forever. And he can do everything for us. Nothing is impossible with him. I faced so many things in my life, I saw so many ups and downs, but he promised me on that night that he will not leave me and he will not forsake me and, really, in every single situation I have found him, he was always there to help me.

80.

I have bipolar disorder. It was diagnosed about twenty years ago and probably been a part of my life since I was a teenager. There was no doubt about all this—I was a fairly obvious case. But what was interesting was that as the medications began to take hold, I started having these momentary flashes of an alternative me. It was literally an alternative reality. The past that was familiar in memory, that I remembered perfectly, didn't exist. I'd lived for years with the wrong past. There was something hallucinatory about it for a while. I mean, I was really scared to talk about it.

I started to investigate the discrepancies, in practical ways. I rang up lots of people and my mother pulled out every passport I'd ever owned and that she'd ever owned while I was on her passport. And my life was as diffuse as I'd thought. But the places where I thought I had been, and had lived lives, did not exist. I'd lived other lives. My whole psyche was littered with delusions and inventions and they were being dissolved by the medication—but not enough of them. And so I was faced with this disturbing mystery of who I really was. And when and where and with whom.

I grew up here, I did this, I went to school here, this was my best friend, my dad and I used to do this on Saturdays. Most people have that. What was discovered with me is that I absolutely do not have that. What became apparent to the doctors—and it wasn't apparent to me—was that the narrative would actually shift. Wherever I was, I had

144

a different set of narratives. So if I lived in England I had a whole set of narratives. And if I lived in America I had a whole set of narratives. And the funny thing is, they were quite complete. Because I *did* go to school in England. And I *did* go to school in America. I did have friends there. None of them knew each other. I just set up a whole new life. That was it [laughs]. People, later in life, would say, *But you just dropped out*. And it was just that I went somewhere else. But being in that sort of manic thing, you know, England stopped: *I'm now in America*. And I would live differently.

What I realised was that this has also influenced my relationship with people, because the reality they had with me, it was not the reality I remembered. If I remembered them at all—in some cases there were people who were very, very close to me for long periods of time, who I didn't remember at all. To sum it up, there are memories I have that I know are real and there are those I suspect or I now know are not. And then there's all these irrecoverable blank spots which are dark or impenetrable. I still hear from others about something I said or did in the past and I have no recollection of it at all. It's like they're talking about a stranger. And this isn't in my old age, this is going back. So you know it comes to this question—what did it really look like? That's why I found the question interesting, and later disturbing.

I chose, a few years ago, because of the damage it was doing to me, to come off medication. And one of the ways I treat myself is to try and imagine what I look like to other people, in the moment. So that I can examine my behaviour as others see it. I can pick up on glitches, moments of mania, which in the past is when I was bloody destructive to my family and so on. So you know the question also became, *What did it look like to others?* I had to see how they saw me and see tics of behaviour as they saw them, not as I imagined them to be. I'm just trying to figure out how I come across, and if it was negative then I'd try and figure that out and change it, or repair it or whatever.

I'm haunted as I get older in terms of, you know, *I wonder what my kids'll think when I'm gone?* I've been a less than ideal husband, I've been a difficult father, I've been an eccentric father, an unfigurable one. And not in particularly enigmatic ways. I still see it in my son—who I'm very close to, and I love and adore—but there's still this moment like, *Which one am I getting today?* I just hope no one judges me too harshly [laughs]. I hope I'm not being too strange for you [laughs]. I hope that I'm coherent for the people I want to be coherent to. Because clearly from my past, even a moment like this where I think I'm being reasonably articulate, it could be absolute bullshit.

81

It's funny how, doing this, my self-consciousness comes and goes in waves.

There's a moment where it's all I can think about—that I'm sitting here recording this, that I'm sitting here doing this weird, slightly mad and embarrassing thing, crouched in the corner of my kitchen next to the window—and I can barely speak. And then suddenly I'm just talking and I don't think about what I'm saying, I just say the thoughts as they come into my head. And for that moment it feels [hesitates]—I dunno. I don't know if it feels like I'm saying anything of any interest, but it feels quite interesting to be speaking without really analysing how that speaking might appear to someone listening to it. Just to speak.

And now another wave of self-consciousness hits and I'm sitting here thinking about the fact that I'm recording this and I'm gonna listen back to it tomorrow and be embarrassed.

But then, as you see, it went quite quickly. In fact, as soon as I start speaking it starts to go because I'm starting to think about my words rather than this thing I call *my self*. And actually, if I could keep talking without a pause, without even thinking, then I don't think I'd feel self-conscious at all.

The sky is clouded tonight, no stars, the light, the ambient light of L_____ bouncing back off it so it seems quite bright, and I saw a heron before when I was leaning out of the window, just maybe ten or twenty minutes ago. A heron flying from _____ up to the reservoir, but now, at night, in the dark. I thought for a moment it was a bat or something, only it didn't move like a bat, of course, it moved like a heron. It's a surprisingly graceful flight for a bird of such an odd shape. All I need to do is keep talking, without thinking, without giving myself space to worry too much about it, and it will all start to come flooding out again and then I will begin to make some sort of progress.

I thought I heard someone.

I think I did.

Or maybe not. It's hard to tell. I actually felt a kind of sick sensation in my stomach and, thinking that, I had a real spike of anxiety.

It's interesting, it never occurred to me that I had anxiety until I was told that I did, and even then I didn't believe it. And eventually I was speaking to, I think to my friend S___ about this diagnosis, and I said I didn't feel anxious, I didn't believe I was suffering from anxiety, and that the only way I could believe it—and this was meant as a joke—was if it turned out that everything I considered normal in the world, every fibre of my existence, was so much built upon anxiety that I didn't even notice or recognise what it was. And actually, it was in that moment that I realised that that was true. That that was indeed the case, that the whole way I operate in the world, the whole of my life, is basically a symptom of anxiety.

I don't know what difference that makes. I mean, in theory you could, I dunno, get some therapy, or start work towards the complete dismantlement of that world. But then, who would you be at the end of it? Who would you be if you dismantled your whole spiritual and emotional world? Would you be the same person? Would you necessarily be a better person? I guess you'd be a less anxious person of course [laughs]. Because that would be what you'd've got rid of. Beyond that, though, I couldn't really say.

Imagine being able to speak without realising you were speaking. Speak, in effect, from some kind of meditative state where you have no consciousness of the words that are coming out. You'd just keep speaking and speaking, it would roll out of your mouth and it would be like a breeze passing through you and leaving behind [hesitates] nothing. The thoughts would come and go and you would have no idea you'd ever had them. And to that extent you never would've done. Because it's the nature of a thought that it's something that you think, surely? If you're not conscious of it, it's not a thought. It would be almost like a trance-like state.

I don't know what I would expect from that. I'm less interested in what it might say or reveal than how that might feel, I suppose. If you could let thought pass through you like a breeze, how would that feel? Well, the clue would be like a breeze, I guess, and actually that's what it's making me think of, that kind of *coldness* at the top of your spine, between your shoulder blades. A kind of coldness that, paradoxically, also feels a bit like sunshine on your back, spring sunshine, so not hot, but just the awareness of it being there.

I have completely lost my track. I can't remember where

that was coming from or where it was leading to. Ah yes, the New Agey tone that I've begun to take since I crouched in the corner of my kitchen, by the windows, looking out, in the dark, whispering into a dictaphone, like a fucking lunatic.

82.

It looked surprisingly peaceful and what it was was my impending death in the next five minutes.

We went to Bali. Everyone wants to go to Bali, don't they? It's on everyone's wishlist. It was like, *Shit, I live in South East Asia—let's go to Bali!* We hired the most ridiculous place I've ever stayed in in my life. It was a giant ethnic house but with Sonos hi-fis, y'know? And a pool and a little gazebo thing by the pool. It had a balcony with proper massage tables with a hole in for your head. It was idyllic. And my plan was basically not to leave the compound, you know what I mean? Just sit by the pool, read some books, stare at the sea. But we have a couple of friends, one's having a hard time, one is just a good friend, and I said, *I've hired this four-room villa with a pool in Bali, do you wanna come along for the ride? Pay your fare, room's yours, just have it cos it's going empty.* Their idea was, *We must see Bali.* And I'm like, *No, I'm really happy with this little twelve foot of Bali in front of me. I've got all the Bali I need!* So they all went off. Actually I would've gone, I wasn't being antisocial. I got stuck doing a pitch with the accountants.

So I'm sitting on my own thinking, *This is great. I don't even mind doing my work.* And then suddenly all of the windows started rattling, really loud. I'm thinking, *Wow, this is an earthquake.* I carry on working. About another five minutes—another one. Things are kind of wobbling and rattling. Like being on a tube train. Same feeling as being on a tube train. Third one. Then there's a fourth one. The fourth one I'm thinking, *Shit, you know what? Maybe I really shouldn't be under the roof?* Because the water is now slopping out of the swimming pool and I'm thinking, *Yeah, this is real, this is an earthquake. Shit!* But I didn't move. I actually stayed under the wooden beams and videoed it for Instagram! How many people have Instagrammed themselves dying? When they get their phone out for whatever's happening, only to discover it's literally the moment of their death?

And then I get this phone call from A__ saying, *You've got to leave.* I'm like, *What?* And she says, *There's a tsunami about to hit.* Normal tsunami timing, should there be such a thing as a timetable, is twelve minutes after the earthquake. Within the next twelve minutes we should start seeing some tsunami action. A__ says, *I'm coming to get you,* and I'm like, *No! No, that's stupid. Don't drive down the mountain.* This is the bit that A__ doesn't like, but this is actually true. A__ said, *Go to the beach and see if the tsunami's coming.* I'm like, *If there is a tsunami coming I'm not sure the beach is the best place I could be!*

And then I thought, in all honesty, in a tsunami it's probably the best place to die—sitting on a beach, rather than dying in a pile of rubble and mud, you know, two hundred yards inland, running away. I just thought, *Well this is it— sit on the beach and then watch it come in and see what happens.* The point of the story is that I actually thought I was going to die. The neighbourhood evacuated, there was an official warning on the news. I thought, *If I am gonna die I could either go upstairs and cling to the balcony in the hope that, you know, the house will stand up and I won't go through the plate glass windows and all of that. Or I can just sit here and wait for it and that's that. My time has come— I'm gonna die.*

So I sat there and forty minutes later A__ turned up. There was no tsunami and I didn't die. But I was very surprised to find out that I accepted the fact that I was probably going to die in a tsunami within ten minutes. And it didn't particularly worry me other than a regret that I wouldn't be with A__. And I found that to be quite comforting, that I didn't have a huge list of things I hadn't done or things I hadn't said, or all that kind of stuff. Or regrets. I thought, *Right now in my life I'm as happy as I can be. And there's nothing I think I should've said to anyone, or I should've done. And if I die, then what a great time to die.* That's what it looked like. It looked peaceful.

I don't think I would've felt like that if I hadn't spent the previous three months annoying the hell out of A__ with my faux-Taoist beliefs. But basically, you kind of fake it till you make it! I've always had a sort of long-felt affinity for Taoists and that sort of thing. And yeah, I think that was the point where it sort of proved itself. I mean, obviously I can't tell you the story had I seen the tsunami, whether my faux-Taoism would've carried the day and I would've sat there watching it come in or whether I would've wet myself, screamed like a child, and started running around. I don't know.

83.

Police brutality isn't just something that happens on a video camera in New York or Atlanta. It also happens off video cameras in Paris and London and Birmingham and Manchester and Austria and Russia. It happens in India, it happens in Australia, it happens all over the world, and it just manifests in different ways.

When I was in my teens, twenties, I probably got stopped on an almost daily basis—questioned or patted down or whatever the case may be. I'm now in this middle life, this middle age, and I'm stopped less. They maybe see a few silver hairs and the beard: *Is he a yout', is he a yout'? Can we stress him and issue different threats to him? Oh no, he might actually complain, he looks like he might know his rights, he might not react aggressively and we haven't got a reason to bend his arms round his back and fit six of us on top of him.*

The last time I got stopped, officially stopped, was the first time in ages, and I'd almost forgot what it was like—*Ah yes, been a while! Welcome back, welcome back!* So yeah, it has been a reality and it didn't need N.W.A for me to tell them that. People aren't saying, *Fuck the firemen*, they're not saying, *Fuck ambulance drivers*, they're saying, *Fuck the police.* The amount of people that I know in London and in Birmingham—as the two main places that I've lived and spent the majority of my life—the amount of people that I know who have been stopped, illegally searched, set up, beat up, arrested, stitched up. Or families that have lost people, and how that affects people. People think it's just one person, they think it's just George Floyd. No. He has brothers, he has children, he has family, he has parents. There's people that are gonna miss this person, there's people that are gonna be anxious, angry, upset, the next time they meet the police. They're not just gonna forget that their loved partner, their loved family member, was murdered on camera.

There's people I've known that are still in jail, from the early nineties, basically for weed. You get stopped, you get into an altercation, then they accuse you of police assault. Somehow you've assaulted six police officers! You must be like Jackie Chan or something, or you must be the world's greatest weed smoker—because weed makes most people relax and chill and wanna sleep and eat a bit of food and watch a film, and somehow you've assaulted six police officers. Then you fight someone in jail, you defend yourself, you're on an attempted murder charge. You spend another ten years and all the time you was in jail for *Oh, we think we smelt marijuana on you.* There's Black men in jail, and there's dispensaries and CBD oil and lip balms and hair treatments made out of hemp.

People have called out racism forever, at least since I've been alive, but I think there's a small spark of people beginning to understand the layers of how this thing affects people. It's not just someone called you a name. It's the job you can get, it's where you live, how you live, how much money you earn, if you're able to get a bank loan or not, how you're represented in media, sports, education, history, biology. Does the doctor listen to you or not when you say you have pain here? Why not? Do they think you're stronger than you are? Do they think you don't feel pain? What's it like not having your own name, your own surname? What does that feel like every time you look at your bank card, or your passport, and you think about it? The majority of diasporic Africans in the Western hemisphere, there's no *Grandad did this* or *Great-grandad did that* for us. We don't know. And then obviously you get back to potential rape and ownership, and things like that. At least the conversation's been had for once.

The mass of Britain is white working-class people. Love the family, come from a culture of drink and working and not thinking—not being allowed to think, not having time to think. The whole feudal set-up, before capitalism is even capitalism, is based on the working classes earning for the higher-ups, and this is still what we're under. We're not allowed to think too deeply or too much. This is why something like philosophy is always laughed at in the mainstream of society, modern society. But you are allowed to drink, drink your troubles away, and see what those guys on the other side of the room are looking at, and if they wanna step outside you are allowed to do that. That is intimacy in this society. That is intimacy. We frown on intimacy, on touch. You have some cultures where men walk arm in arm and hand in hand. And they're usually more chilled, those cultures—not the countries, but those cultures. Don't start wars, they don't have prisons, they don't have that much violence, they don't have that much theft. These are some of the oldest cultures in the world. I'm talking about people like the San people in Central and Southern Africa. Fifty, sixty, seventy thousand years old. Y'know, they might know a few things [laughs] by now! This is older than Greece, older than Egypt, older than Rome, definitely older than modern Britain and USA. Have a look at them.

84.

My mum and dad had a pretty rocky marriage. I mean, it was a shotgun wedding, when my mum got pregnant with my brother, and they probably never should've got together. But in 196_ it was what you did. So they got together and I came along, four years later. But they had a pretty turbulent marriage and she was suffering from a lot of post-natal illness. I think she had post-natal psychosis, to be honest, after she had me. And a lot of early memories were just of those two arguing, basically, and having massive rows. He would leave for a bit and then he would come back and try and make it work, and then he would leave. And obviously at the time, being a kid, I didn't really understand what was happening—I just wanted him to stay. But eventually, when I was about six and my brother was about ten, he ended up leaving and he went missing.

I can remember everyone being really worried and nobody knowing where he was. And this seemed to go on for quite a long time. Then one evening the police came and—I mean, I was only young, so I'm not sure of the exact timeline of events—the neighbours, like the friendly neighbours, were in the lounge as well, and I was in the lounge. And it turns out they'd worked out that he'd taken his own life and he was actually at the end of our garden, in the garage. He'd switched on the engine and died from the fumes of the car. So that was a pretty shocking thing. More shocking, obviously, now, thinking back. For that time that he was missing he was actually dead at the end of the garden.

I can remember the police being there and eventually it came to light that they'd found him and he was dead. My mum being hysterical and all the neighbours crying and my brother crying. And I can remember feeling confused. Because I kinda knew that I should be crying but I didn't really fully understand the weight of what somebody dying meant. I was just sitting there, looking around. And I can remember I started to pretend to cry. Because I just thought, *Oh, everyone's crying, I should be crying, so I better start crying, too.* I started kind of closing my eyes and just doing a few fake sobs, feeling completely and utterly bewildered by it all and not really knowing how I should feel. So obviously that was pretty traumatic. But at the time it just felt really strange.

Fast forward many, many years later. I think I was probably in my late twenties and because of my chaotic, turbulent childhood, I was looking for different types of therapy to help me. I found this hypnotherapist that was recommended to me, he was in the King's Road. I remember it being the far end of King's Road, down where Malcolm McLaren and Vivienne Westwood's shop used to be, down that end. And I went to see this guy and he was a bit strange but he seemed to be powerful, to have some quite strong powers. He managed to put me in a trance by saying a few words—there was no watches being swung in front of my face or anything else. And I think I've got quite a suggestive mind anyway. He was talking to me about traumas and so forth and I told him about this situation. He said, *If you like, I can take you back there and we can do some work on it.* And I thought, *Okay, this is interesting.* Obviously a bit scary as well. But he put me in a trance and he took me back and he said, *Okay, I want you to be outside the window of the lounge where it all happened.*

And I was, it was as clear as day, it was like being in a video game, it was like 4K ultra-real—*I was there.* The grass was under my feet, I was looking through the window of my old house. And I could see me, I could see my brother, I could see the neighbours, I could see the police, all inside the house. He said, *Okay, I want you to go in now.* So I walked into the front door, turned right into the lounge and I could see everything! We had this white vinyl sofa, I could see all the nick-nacks, I could see the decorations, I could see everything. It was amazing. Truly amazing. I don't know how much my mind is creating this and filling in the blanks or whether we truly remember everything and it's all stored away, but it was incredibly real. He said, *Okay, I want you to go and sit next to yourself.* Which was pretty weird [laughs]. But I couldn't do much about it cos I was in a trance, so I did. I went and sat down on this sofa, next to this little blond-haired boy of six. And [the therapist] said, *Now I want you to comfort yourself.* So I put my arms around myself and I comforted this small, confused child. It was really profound. It really did something. I'm not saying it cured me of all my neuroses and psychoses, whatever it is that I've got. But it was so powerful and so profound and so strange and so real. It was, yeah, a truly amazing experience. And I'm glad I did it.

85

I'm one of six kids. Typically Irish Catholic family. And
I come from the countryside in Ireland, just south of the
border, actually. Literally just a couple of miles south of the
border. My parents didn't have much education but they're
both kind of driven. My mum started doing markets in
the eighties—before markets were cool! She would make
loads of stuff—cushions, curtains and anything to do with
haberdashery—on the big Singer sewing machine all day
long and all night long. And we were all like little elves, you
know, helping to stuff cushions, cut curtain tape, whatever.
And then we used to go to these big markets. I worked on
markets from when I was about six years of age. You'd have
a lot of Asian people doing markets and you'd have Gypsies
doing markets. Didn't have a lot of normal families doing
markets, if we could be described as a normal family, but it
was a really fun environment to grow up on. Hard-working
as well. Massively hard-working. Market life is hard. It was
so different, basically, to all my friends around me whose
parents had normal jobs or normal lives and all that kind of
stuff.

My mum'd go away to fairs in the summertime. There
used to be these big fairs back in Ireland in the eighties, when
Ireland was not such a rich country. You'd have these fairs
and people'd come out that one day that year, all the kids
from the countryside, farmers, whatever, come to get their
sheets, come to get their year's supply of things. So Mam'd

go to these markets and make an absolute killing. But we always had to go, we'd all have to pile into a van.

This one time me and my sister went with her, and her and my aunt were in the front of the van. She'd also obviously want to get as much stuff into the van as possible. It was filled to the brim. There was about a foot, a foot and a half between all the products and the roof of the van. It was so dangerous. Big plastic bags full of cushions, which are all full of polyester. The most dangerous thing in the world, like. And my mum was probably having a cigarette in the front seat. We had to lie flat like that the whole way on the trip. You know, the four hours over there. If she had've braked really suddenly the two of us would've been like [flying noise]—straight through the front window [laughs]. Nobody thought anything at the time! You just got in and got on with it. And we travelled four hours across the west of Ireland to the middle of nowhere. There was supposed to be a big farmers' market the next day. Well, we got there in the middle of the night. Me and my sister were sleeping in the back, and everybody just fell asleep in the dark.

We woke up the next morning, at about six in the morning. And we were literally surrounded, the whole van surrounded by cows. Cows as far as you could see [laughs]. And loads of Irishmen speaking in Irish, loads of farmers, just all speaking about it. They hadn't even knocked on the window to say, *Do you wanna move on?* or anything like that. They just went about their business. All around us. I don't know whether they were afraid of speaking to a couple of women in a van or what it was, but it was really funny. It was just crazy, the pain that we went through for them to do their business. The rest of that day, I remember that it was so windy and the whole thing was blown everywhere. It was a whole farce, basically.

I ended up working on a stall for Casio watches. I used to sell Casio watches, back in the early nineties, when I was twelve, fixing people's Casio watches and changing the straps, taking the batteries out. I used to have my own stall selling books. I used to sell Mills and Boons. I didn't know what they were, all I knew was all the old ladies loved them. I'd sell them three for a pound and I used to make a fortune, used to come home with thirty quid in my pocket at the end of the day. They would just be buying 'em, buying 'em, buying 'em. Or I'd go and pick fruit and sell it. I'd stand there with all my clear bags and my fruit and the weighing scales, and call out, *Half a kilo of damsons for five pounds!* It feels like another world. Better than doing a paper round, I guess.

There was a dark side of it, too, because, you know, we missed out on a lot of childhood things a lot of the time. We now look back, you know, we talk about it among ourselves. You always felt you had to go to work for the firm. There was definitely an obligation on it. When me and my sisters look back we laugh so much about it. They have got their own kids, like teenage kids. They're like, *Can you imagine asking them now to get into a van full of cushions and then lie down flat for four hours and then wake up in the middle of nowhere?!* We didn't even moan about it. It's hard to cut my parents down for that because they were redeeming themselves from really humble, harsh upbringings. So you can't go, *Oh, you stole my childhood!* And I made up for it in my twenties!

86.

I used to have a little muntjac visit me for about fourteen years, come down every morning. What did it look like? Beautiful. Totally weird little creature. Stocky. They're always quite stocky and chunky, they remind me of a boar–deer cross. We get quite a lot of roe here, and they're quite gangly. One or two young ones at the moment look like llamas.

I live in a caravan, have done for twenty years now. Right in the middle of what was until recently a hundred-year-old orchard, a traditional orchard. It's very remote, very detached, how I need it, really, cos I don't get on with people. Need to be quite isolated. Cos I'm mental, basically [laughs]. They can't decide what—autism, ADHD seem to be the things. Met the deer on the first day we moved in, but it took him probably six years to introduce himself and start demanding, and then one day he was just camped outside my door, and I knew he wasn't going anywhere till I fed him. I fed him these sort of nuts that you put in a bird feeder, mixed with some Alpen, like grain. But he didn't just want feeding, he wanted scratching. He liked it under the jowl, behind the horns where he couldn't get. It was quite an intimate relationship, especially the last six, seven years. Very interesting little creature.

He wasn't alone, he had a missus, or an ex-missus. We called her Split Lip, cos she had a strange split lower lip, and she was probably the first one to try and get food. She used to stare with her weird lazy eye, looking through the window.

I used to duck down to try and avoid her, cos I didn't wanna give away my food at the time [laughs]. I couldn't believe I was crouched down behind my sink, trying not to be spotted by a deer. My partner named him Big Boy, so we called him Biggie. There was Little Man, who was his son, and there was Big Boy, which was him. He was quite the bully to his son, and chased him off within the first few years. I used to camp out with him. We used to sit on the grass and I'd just put my arm over his body. Got videos of all of this, I've got some nice videos up close, and my partner captured some nice videos. And he knew when I was round at her place. He'd come and get me. He'd stand in front of her window like, *Is he in there? Come on, get him out, I want a scratch, I'm hungry.*

He died and it was quite a shock. He was about twenty-four. He was here for four years before I turned up. They're only supposed to live for about seven years. He was very well kept but his last few years were quite bad. He got hurt, there was a new deer on the cards and he had his mouth ripped open. Then he had his eye gouged out. I could tell he couldn't see, cos I could see him in the dark, and there was a weird distortion to his retina. I knew he was gonna die. He come down one day, and he walked off, and it was different to all the other times. That's going back about three years ago now. It really changed life for me. I didn't realise it. It was a shock to lose him, and it made me really angry. I actually went around looking for the biggest guys that I could to have a fight with. I didn't realise it at the time but it was quite self-destructive, obviously. Cos I would've had my arse handed to me [laughs]. I was convinced he was killed by a local guy. I found a guy walking around in the woods at the back in camo, and I thought, *I bet you fucking shot him, didn't you?* I had visions about sticking this muntjac horn up his throat, in this ironic death [laughs].

You get an MOT check at fifty and the doctors asked me some questions, and said, *You're really angry. What's up?* And I went on to say, *I lost this deer, but I can't justify it, cos it wasn't my pet, it was just a three times daily little meeting with him.* I think the doctors were quite good. I saw a therapist at the doctor's at that time, and she said, *It's totally acceptable, this beast chose you, you didn't go out and choose it from a selection of creatures, it came down and forced itself on you, so don't beat yourself up about losing something that you had an obvious friendship with.* He was a big part of my life, being that I'd been here twenty years, and that was fourteen of it, and I think that played a big part. I mean, I dropped out of all work in 2004 cos I had a weird little breakdown, but I'd try to fit until then, if you know what I mean, I'd always try to sort of fit, so ending up here and ending up in a weird relationship with a deer was on the cards, I guess.

Over the last five or six years, maybe seven, something happened in my mind. I dunno what it was. I'd done with therapy, and I'd pulled back, and I think it was all coming together. My mate, can't remember where he was coming from, I think he was living on Shetland at the time, but he come through Achnahaird in Scotland. He'd picked a load of mushrooms on his way down. He must've picked about a thousand mushrooms and we had five hundred each. He lost his shit that night, big time. He was saying, *I can't walk, I can't walk, I've had it, I've had it.* And I was just like, *Oh, for fuck's sake, I was really enjoying myself here, feeling rooted to the ground,* but no. That was the last one we done, but it done something to me. I found a core, as it were. And all my troubles, everything, they were satellites and I was the planet. I was the central thing. Everything was much more manageable after that. But it still took a few years.

87

It was right in that point in winter when the days are really short, and it was raining all the time and suddenly the atmosphere became really heavy and I started to ache across my shoulders. And then it got worse and worse. Things started closing in. The house gradually became a darker place. We couldn't eat. I couldn't eat, barely at all. I was forcing myself to eat bits and bobs. The darkness that had descended on the house just got darker. I started not being able to sleep at night. I felt wired the whole time. I started taking Night Nurse, which helped—it kind of knocks you out—but then after about three days of taking that, it didn't work anymore.

After about six days of this I just started crying all the time. Everything looked or felt sad. Anything. _____'s sister bought a dog chew for our dog and sent it over. [It] was a doll, and it was Priti Patel and I got obsessed with this fucking thing. I said, in the end, *You've gotta put that thing away because it's making me feel so sad.* She was like, *It's just a toy.* I was like, *I know, I can't explain it, but it makes me feel really sad to see it on the floor.* I dunno whether I imagined it or what, but I thought my skin had turned yellow. I couldn't get comfortable, I couldn't lie down, I couldn't sit up, I couldn't roll over. I was constantly agitated. I had to keep moving around because everything felt uncomfortable. My temperature was going all over the place, so we had to open the window. But then every time we opened the window, this smell came in, which I don't think existed, but it existed for me. Every time we opened the window it was like raw sewage smell, unbearable.

I was losing proper cognition, I think. One of the reasons I couldn't sleep, which is very common, there's a feeling that *If I go to sleep, I'll stop breathing*. Because it's an effort to breathe. But also, every time I closed my eyes, I had fucking ghosts or something around me. They were like doctors or something. I'd close my eyes and there'd be people standing over me, all around me, poking me and prodding me and doing stuff to me. Every time I closed my eyes. That got worse in hospital, obviously [laughs]—because it was happening anyway. But every time I closed my eyes, I had fucking *bad actors* prodding me. It was totally bizarre. It just carried on in that way until I started saying, *I can't cope anymore. I don't feel like I can cope. I don't think I'm going to make it through this. Everything looks too bleak*. I was bursting into tears eight times a day, you know, over nothing. Everything seemed really hopeless. And at the same time, my physical symptoms were getting worse.

Which is when we called the ambulance. They came out and they looked at me and they were like, *He's borderline. The situation's quite bad at the hospital at the moment, we've got very strict rules about who we're bringing in and who we're not*. So they told me to stay at home. That was on Christmas Day. And then I got worse overnight. So the next day, _____ rang them up and explained what was going on, and they said, *Just bring him down*. So she took me in. And then when they saw me, they just said, *Right, he's gotta stay here.* I was terrified. I mean, on the one hand, I was like, *At least if I stop breathing there'll be people here who can try and help.* Because that was one of my main concerns at that point—that I would stop breathing. And actually, as soon as they put the oxygen mask on me, it felt easier to breathe. So there was a definite sense of relief. But mentally, the ten hours or whatever I spent in A&E was so disturbing. People were wailing, people were crying. The woman in the bed next to me was dying and the nurse was having to hold the phone up to her ear and it was her daughter hysterically going, *PLEASE DON'T LEAVE US.* I could hear every word. I was just left in a bed, watching this guy opposite me who had it and then had a stroke whilst he was ill with it, and was just throwing up all over the place. And I was just [laughs] trying to go to a happy place.

And then they got me into a ward. But the feeling of absolute hopelessness [stayed]. Because it wasn't just that I felt hopeless about my situation, in that I might not make it or whatever—I became hopeless about everything, about the world. I spent whole nights thinking about every mistake I'd ever made in my life and why I should have done this and why didn't I do that? Putting this whole negative spin on everything that had happened to me up to that point. It was an obsession, you know, starting to think, *It doesn't matter if I do survive—everything's fucked anyway.* Everything looked sad. I was so sick of lying in bed all the time and I thought if I made it to the window, that might cheer me up. I got there and it was like everything was tainted, everything

172

looked dark and foreboding—the sea, everything. It was just overpowering.

I've since found out this wasn't just me. This is how it affects a lot of people. It fucks with your mind. I felt disembodied, literally. At worst I felt like I'd been invaded. I've talked quite a lot to the woman up the road about her experience, cos she got very ill as well. She was like, *I felt like I'd been invaded by evil spirits. I felt like my body wasn't my own.* And I was like, *Fuck, so did I.* That feeling of being poisoned. My body wasn't my own. It's like your personality is being squashed out of the picture and this thing's taking over. I haven't thought about it like that before, but that's exactly what it felt like. It felt like I was being pushed out of the picture. And this other thing was taking over. And it was a poisonous thing. I was trying to hang on. I had this tiny voice, but it was getting smaller and smaller. Well, it wasn't a voice. It was me. It was like I was retreating into this tiny place in the back of my mind while all this other shit took over.

And then gradually as my symptoms lifted, I started to feel better. For a while I was paranoid that I wasn't. It was so slow. There were moments where people would remind me: *Yeah, but you did this today and imagine, you never woulda done that even last week.* And I'd be like, *Oh yeah, of course. I must be getting better.* Because it was so slow. I think, to be honest, it was probably the first time I had sex when I thought, *Oh yeah, I can do that again.* There's something quite life-affirming about it. And you think, *Ah. Actually maybe everything isn't broken.*

88.

Oh, it's one of my favourite words. Like on my Tinder it says 'slut4slut', because I want to make it clear that I just really love sex [laughs]. It's like a term of endearment in my house. I have for years written emails to people saying, *Hey slut!* I call my sister Slag instead of her name and [when] I send her mail, I change her name so that *slag* is in her last name every time, but in a different way [laughs]. So I just really like calling people a slut [laughs]. There has definitely been a reclamation. I think a huge part of that, certainly in the queer community, is the book *The Ethical Slut*. I mean, it's a great book, but it's boring. Polyamory and ethical non-monogamy have become the veganism of modern society. They just wanna tell you all about it and I don't care. I just want people to have sex with who they want to have sex with and have a nice time. But I don't always want to hear about it. And I certainly don't want people to approach me and say, *Do you know I'm poly?* And I'm like, *Well, of course you are. You've got a man-bun and you look a bit pale—are you vegan, too? Yes, of course you are. Have you been to a sex party? Yes. Are you going to tell me about it? Yes. Do I want any of that? No.* I've been to my share of orgies, I've been to dungeons, but I don't need to tell anyone about it.

[But] I suppose the only description for my relationship currently is ethical non-monogamy. I've probably got my little list around somewhere. We sat down and wrote some guidelines for ourselves, fully in the acknowledgement that we were gonna break them, because that's what happens when you have boundaries—you wanna test them. But we sat down and decided that we don't have any interest in having a romantic relationship with anyone else. And so we are emotionally monogamous, but otherwise sexually open. And that's fun cos I think a lot of our fantasies, both shared and individually, involve anonymity and quite a lot of people. The pandemic's been really bad for these fantasies. It's very hard to enact it [laughs]. I don't mind, cos the relationship I have is such a core part of my life and my being that I feel very happy and content and I don't need anything else. Of course I *desire* other things but, I dunno, it just feels a bit greedy! And I don't want to endanger either myself or anyone else because of those desires. It's fine. But for me, it creates a great sense of safety and security. Once you can get away from this idea that you should only be having sex with one person and that's the person you love, you can then have these really rich experiences with other people.

I spent a lot of my twenties being told by women that I behaved like a man. And I didn't like that very much because I found that reductive. I found that quite misogynistic. Particularly with heterosexual sex, there was this baseline assumption that there are roles that are defined, which are that if you are having straight sex, the man will be dominant and the woman will be submissive. And I found over time that that made me really angry and it made me really scared. And I didn't like it. I was married to someone who had some sadistic tendencies that he thought were just a normal branch of male sexuality. And I was like, *No, no. No, no. That's something you need to talk about with people! That's quite messed up.* And no kink-shaming, but you should be able to define it as one. You should not be able to say, *Oh, well, everyone else I've done this with has liked it.* You should be able to say, *I have these interests and these fetishes and these drives that some people may not respond well to.* There just needs to be a conversation around it. Specifically stuff around choking and violence—to an excessive degree that probably came from porn. It meant in that relationship I was never allowed to express my sexuality in the way that I wanted to. We had an open-ish marriage and I would go and hook up with women or more queer people and found that I could then express myself in a way that felt comfortable and was able to have the sort of power exchange that interested me rather than one that I felt threatened and unsafe because of. There's an inherent element of suppression and control within straight sexuality, which is disappointing, and it's to do with the patriarchy and it's to do with the fact that, you know, it was still legal to rape your wife until 1992 in the UK, or something like that. There's a lot that gets contained within straightness that is not spoken of enough. I find that it's just a way of enacting trauma on people—often who've already been traumatised. I would say one thing that I find quite telling about most of the queers I know is that everyone's experienced some sort of trauma, mostly at the hands of men. And I'm not shitting on men, because I love them. But the system around masculinity is toxic, and if you follow all of the paths that you're told to follow, you can end up in quite a dangerous place for other people's safety and well-being.

After I got divorced I was like, *I'm not going to date anyone that isn't queer and I'm not gonna date anyone that isn't in therapy.* With my ex, if I hooked up with a woman, he's like, *Great, now I can.* I was like, *It's not a like-for-like system.* It was always about power. No, it's not a competition. But now I think, yeah, to have that comfort in the fact that we both know that there are certain things we're not going to be able to give each other, but then there's no difficulty in going and doing this with other people. And I mean, one of the things I discovered about myself, which perhaps was unsurprising, was that I really love pegging men! It's a great thing to discover—and there's loads who want it. I've always had this uncertainty about, *Well, am I like a man, as all of these people have told me? And am I wrong to want to be in charge?* The answer is no. I'm just fucking the wrong people. You find the people that want to have someone else be in charge. I dom-ed a bit, which was just so much fun. I was kind of like a backup dom! My friend, she goes on paid dates in the Bay Area—a lot of that was just incredibly wealthy, badly dressed men in their thirties needing 'a woman' to agree to go to a public place with them so that they could be perceived to be normal. So she made a lot of money going to the mall with men who bought her thousands of dollars of stuff. If she ever had any uncertainty about going to someone's house to go and dom them, she would invite me.

And then that just felt safer. And obviously, like, fine, I got paid. But more than anything, it was just really, really fun. And also, they loved being shouted at in a British accent! I don't know that that's something I would want to do on my own, but it felt really fun as a group activity: *Oh, we're going to make some money, humiliating a man sexually for an hour? Great! What more could I ask for? Sounds like a dream.*

89.

There were more and more camps at different gates. And each of the camps took on their own personalities. They were all colours of the rainbow. The main gate was Yellow, the main gate to the base, that had the original camp. But there started to be far too many women to live just at one camp. And so women broke away and set up other camps. They were usually groups of women that knew each other. And there was some sort of theme to it, for want of a better word. I can't even remember them all now. There were quite a lot of women there who were religious, who were mainly Christian and were there for spiritual reasons. And they set up a camp and then that camp attracted more women who thought along the same lines. [So] Orange was the religious one. And then there was the sort of radical feminist separatist gate where they didn't even allow male visitors— no men were allowed down the path approaching the camp. Green was that separatist one. And one of the others was Blue, which we used to joke that we'd set up there because it was the closest one to the local pub! There was a pub that you could walk to from Blue Gate. Because the base was very large. I think it was about twenty miles around the perimeter fence. It wasn't just like a little field that you could see all the way round. I ended up at Blue Gate, where we were mostly vegan but liked to be in walking distance of the pub, and a few sort of New Agey types were there, for want of a better description. I'm not sure what our label was, it wasn't quite so clearly defined as some of the others. But anyway, that was where I settled.

Once you settled in a gate, then you sort of had a smaller group that you identified with—a lot. Whereas the camp at the main gate, it was starting to get too big for everyone to know each other very well. So it was good. But also strategically, it meant that we had camps at all of the gates and we could keep an eye on what they were doing. Because the constant theme was, you know, *How can we disrupt the daily life of the base?* You know, by either cutting the bolts on the gates so they couldn't lock the gates, or lying in the road in front of some important vehicles that they were trying to get in to deliver something, or just generally making a nuisance of ourselves at any time of day or night. It was hard for them to deal with us, because we could be anywhere or everywhere. They never knew what we were doing. And because the perimeter fence was so long, they couldn't possibly patrol all of it. They did patrol, twenty-four hours a day, but they hadn't got enough personnel. You only had to watch the patrol going past and you knew nobody else would be coming by for quite a long time. You didn't have to be a sort of experienced spy type. It was quite easy to see when there was going to be a gap and then to cut a hole in the fence and go in and do a bit of spray-painting, or a bit of damage to show you'd been there. And really the point of it was not just to be a nuisance—it was to show that it wasn't a safe place to keep nuclear weapons. Because if we could get in—a bunch of untrained women with just a few tools that we'd bought down the local hardware shop—that to us made it obvious that it wasn't a safe place to keep nuclear weapons.

Things were decided by consensus. The meetings round the campfires where decisions needed to be made—about how to use the limited money that we'd got from donations or when to plan a big action—these decisions could take hours and days because it was true consensus decision-making. You just went on and on and on until everybody was happy with the decision, even if it wasn't quite what they wanted to start with. It was an important process so that nobody felt ignored or nobody felt that their voice hadn't been heard. It was a process that I'd never witnessed anywhere. I'd only ever worked in hierarchical settings—you know, in school, in education and then later in a job. The idea of not having a leader was a very interesting one. Actually putting that into practice. At that time the camp was in the news a lot and journalists used to come, or TV reporters, and they used to say, *Who's the leader? Who should we speak to?* And we used to say, *Well, you can speak to anybody. Cos we haven't got a leader.* And they couldn't get their heads around the fact that actually nobody was in charge of anything. *Oh, but who's in charge of press coverage?* The reverse of that is seeing that if there's no structure and no leadership, then it must be chaotic and hopeless. I think that a lot of people wrote off the chances of the camp doing anything because they saw it as being quite chaotic. And they didn't see that actually that was a really important thing that was going on, as well as the protest—that we were all learning a different way to be. A different way to live.

And there was a huge range of women there. Some of us already thought of ourselves as feminists long before we went there but other women didn't at all, had not got any sort of concept of a feminist movement or a women-only movement. That was still quite a new idea in those times. And some women had pitched up at the camp having left awful things behind. I remember somebody coming from I think it was D_____. She'd just suddenly up and left her violent husband and come to the camp cos somebody had told her about it. She was desperate, you know. She'd fled this very difficult, abusive relationship and she'd pitched up there. And she found it very difficult at first because she didn't really know anything about feminism or about the women's [movement]. I think she'd seen it as a handy place she could escape to. But actually she lived there for years. Something about the way we were living and the way we were looking after each other was attracting women that were living in difficult situations. That gave rise to a lot of long-winded consensus decisions to be made [laughs]. Because it was difficult—obviously we wanted to support any woman that wanted to come and take part, but it was quite difficult if women were needing a lot of support. Cos that was important, but it also wasn't what we were gone there to do.

It's actually quite hard work keeping going at a camp. Everybody's got to eat. Everybody's got to have a way to get washed, to wash their clothes, somewhere to sleep. It's a huge operation. In the summer it's all lovely. You can sleep under the stars. You can just throw a bucket of water over yourself in the woods. But in the winter, when you're breaking the ice to try and get a kettle of water on the fire, trying to get the fire lit, and everybody's waiting an hour for the first cup of tea of the day, actually it's quite hard. It's not romantic living in the camp in the winter. And the council are sending in the bailiffs to evict the camp every week and everything's getting torn down, and you've got to build it all up again. So it was quite hard living there, especially in the winter months.

There's quite a lot of days that stand out in my mind, like the first time I took part in a blockade there, blockading the gate, and the police came and dragged us all away one by one. I was quite scared because I'd certainly never been manhandled by the police in my life. Whereas you end up quite casual about it. And also I think the adrenaline boosts you through these things. So when you're lying on the road or blockading the gate or whatever, you do end up quite high. And that carries you through. And of course there was always a lot of singing and chanting and I think you always felt like you were in it together. And that you were looking out for each other. And that made it possible to do all sorts of things that you wouldn't have thought about doing on your own. There was that feeling that if there was another G_____ woman around, they'd got your back. Always. I still have that feeling of solidarity.

90.

The biggest impact on my life was deciding not to fly back
from New York City on September 11 2001 and instead
fly back on September 10 2001. I looked at the screen and
hovered over the dates, deciding which day I wanted to come
back. And I picked the same flight but a day earlier. It was
chance. I just remember looking at it and thinking, *What day
shall I go?* On September 10 I flew back, landed, went to the
gym, switched on the telly, and the Twin Towers was coming
down. And September 10, the last place I went to was the
Twin Towers. I went from the Twin Towers to the airport, to
London to watch them fall down. Giddy. Dizzy. Didn't really
know what to make of it. I just thought, *Is this real? Is this
for real?* And then suddenly my phone started to ring. And
everybody wanted to know where my cousins were and if I
was alright. Then it was just action stations after that.

Eventually, I felt angry and I felt sad. I felt angry because
this is what happens to normal people who don't make
these decisions, who don't get into weird alliances for wars,
for energy or fuel or just the unending desire to be rich.
It doesn't affect those people who make those decisions,
it affects the average person in the street—on either side.
And every time I see that, it makes me angry. We had
twenty years of non-stop war after that. And who benefited
from it? Some people got rich! Some people got more rich.
Some people got more rich and they don't give a shit about
anyone. Certain people got more rich, lots of people died,

lots of innocent people died. So I guess it makes me think about that, it makes me think about power and how it's got divorced from morality. And that's a problem.

A lot of my family lived and still do live in New York and I spend a lot of time there. So watching the American people consider the American Dream when you know that it might not be true, it's definitely been the soundtrack to my life. In Britain that's what we live in, isn't it? What it feels like is being a bystander in a slow-motion car crash. We're standing there in a mix of horror and glee. And all the while, the wheels are falling off. Or, you know, your legs are falling off. As you're watching it [laughs]. And, you know, the Overton window's just moved so much. This is incredible. We've got people who are clearly not fit for any office in the highest office in the world, lying to our faces. It's just a blatant disrespect. Like, I'm watching the stuff today. Come on, you got sick, now you're doing doughnuts in the car park. You can barely stand but you're pulling off the mask—what is this shit?! It's insane.

There's this new strategy, this new strand of political thought and political action, which is to just lie. Directly, bareface, blatantly, like raw power, just lie until it's true. All the most powerful people in the world, or the world powers, seem to be engaged in that. Subjugating their civilians. And I struggle with it because you oscillate between feeling powerless and then feeling like if you just completely dip out of it then you're letting it happen. I think humanity, at present, it feels like we're in this perfect stasis, where acting feels completely futile. And futility feels normal. It's this continuous extinguishing of hope by bombarding people with information. So you're constantly second-guessing what's true and what isn't. And you're driven by trying to understand what's going to happen, not by what we really want to happen. Reality seems reactive. Basic things that just seem so simple are made unnecessarily hard. And I can't understand why you would make them hard. And those things seem to be increasing. Hopefully it's just a cycle and soon enough they'll be decreasing and it won't feel so distraught? I mean, maybe it's the end of the world? I think it might be. But when I say that I think it might just mean the end of certain ways of thinking or certain ways of being that don't really make sense? Surely nothing stays the same?

I mean, this is it. 2020, what've we had? We've had coronavirus, bush fires, we've had aliens, we've had war, we've had locusts. You know when they have the end-of-the-world movies? And they have the montage of *This is how the apocalypse happened* before the *Mad Max* desert? I never thought we would actually live through that montage. I might make a film of all the proto-apocalypse montages in one long movie. So it never gets to the actual post-disaster barren wasteland. It's just all disaster. A single loop of endless apocalypse. Maybe this current news cycle is that endless loop. When you think about it, twenty-four-hour bad news—isn't that just the endless apocalypse already? It already exists.

So, yeah, we started off with luck, this moment that I felt lucky because I made a decision that only I knew about, this interruption of my reality. But if I'd never known, I'd be none the wiser, obviously. Probably finished my workout, to be fair. I woulda been a bodybuilder. And I'd have a mock-Tudor semi somewhere and loads of medals in mint condition, an XR3i and, I dunno, a body oil endorsement. And dogs, loads of big dogs.

I like dogs, I love dogs, but I'm not sure about big ones. My girlfriend really wants a big dog and she's really small. Big dogs shit big shits. What do you want that for? In my head, I wanna kind of minimise the size and weight of the dog shits that I have to handle. And she's a small person, so the ratio is ridiculous. She'll have to walk around with armfuls of dog shit. I try and think about everything. I try to think about everything really, really extra, extra logical. And then immediately try and completely discard that and just be as whimsy as possible. And then after that, I'm internally ecstatic with my chaos creation. So I'll explain to her why we shouldn't get a big dog and, you know, draw the big-shit graphic and everything. Then when she says, *Oh, but I really want a big dog*, I say, *YEAH!* And then I go and get the biggest dog we can find, for the biggest shit we can find, right? And then kind of laugh at the ensuing nonsense. It's that logic/chaos thing, isn't it? That oscillation of different extremes. There's no middle ground for me. Just one or zero. Everything else doesn't exist. One or minus one. I don't like tepid water, it's gotta be hot or cold. Not really into neutral things. I don't like IKEA. It makes my head hurt, my sinuses hurt. I think blandness quite frightens me. Makes me think that someone's not telling the truth. I can't really put my finger on it. I watched *Come Dine with Me* the other day and this woman was on there and she said, *Oh, I don't like food that's too tasty* [laughs]. *I don't like food that tastes too much.* I'm like, *Whaat??!* I'm not saying you've got to eat wheels of blue cheese every day or just lick salt for fun. But she doesn't like food that tastes of anything.

I still feel hope. That's the thing. That's the conundrum—I still feel hopeful. I still feel hope in my heart. I'm weirdly optimistic. Cos I love everything. I used to put on clubs and I'd go and stand in the corner when everyone was in there having a good time. I'd stand there with my hood on or whatever, just enjoying, gaining pleasure. I'd watch people smiling and dancing and I'd imagine their lives. Imagine what it was like and what they do for a job, you know? What their parents looked like and, if they were gonna get together, what their kids would look like. I got pleasure from their pleasure. I guess I'd just feel really human, just really connected to other people. And so that's what I like.

91

I think doctors have a funny idea about death, because we see
a lot of it. I mean, my first job as a houseman was looking
after a little girl with leukaemia who was dying. And it was
the start of parents staying in, so not only was there the
little child dying but I had the mother to contend with, too,
with her grief. I was twenty-two and only just qualified and
I wasn't really able to. So one becomes actually hardened
over the years, to death. You establish an idea that death is
there. I see it as an eventuality. When you're born you've got
an eventual death that's earlier or later. You can't extend it
forever. It's going to happen. I do think you have a very odd
idea about general mortality. How you feel about your own
mortality, of course, is quite different.

I don't actually think very much about it but I suppose
I'm hopeful, like everybody else, that if one's gonna die, you
just die. It's that drag out towards death that is so difficult,
isn't it? That's the thing people always worry about and I'm
no different from anybody else in thinking that. I mean, I
do still think about getting some sort of pill. Even more so
now. It would be much easier, wouldn't it? I don't really see
why we can't sort something out like that. The difficulty
might be that, as you got more demented, you might not
know where you'd kept it. So you'd be looking for the pill.
That's always a bit of a drawback. The idea of getting it
on the internet worries me—that it actually won't work.
Wouldn't it be dreadful if you took it and then you woke up

the next morning and you were still there? Or half killed?

I'm not looking forward to the dying bit. The dying. I don't mean the dead bit. If I never woke up I'd think that was really great. And the same if your father did, too. I mean, I'd be upset but I'd think, *Gosh, that was just what he wanted.* It is that dragging out. And I do think we do rather drag it out now. I mean, they operate on people in their nineties. I can't see the point. Why don't they just let them die? Partly it's the relatives, of course. The idea that you get used to the idea they're dying. The fact you've had time to adjust. I think whatever you do, death is something where you're going to say, *I wish I'd said this* or *I wish I'd done this.* Because it's so final, isn't it? There's no way you can recompense for the bit you didn't say, even if you had a long time. A shock is worse for the relatives but better for the person. They're not going to be regretting what they didn't say because they're not there anymore.

[My mother] used to say, every time we'd come and visit, *Can you get me some pills?* I couldn't, because I was a doctor. Originally when she had a stroke I said, *I don't want a drip up or anything.* She was unconscious and she wasn't in any pain. But they wouldn't do it until [my sister] came back. They kept the drip up until they came back and then of course she woke up. And then lived I don't know how many years—half lived. I was relieved, really, when she died eventually. Interestingly, I don't really remember much about my father's dying. And I don't quite know why. He had a stroke when I was seventeen, the first stroke, and that was quite traumatic. He was only sixty-two. And then he got a bit better and lived on until he was seventy. I think he had another stroke and died. I remember at work they kept telling me to take time off and I said, *I don't really need to take time off.* And I didn't go down there and I didn't go to see Ma until I went to the funeral. It was an odd reaction, really.

I think I might prefer it for me to die first. I always think I'll probably die first because I've got more reasons to drop down dead than he has. Probably that's a purely selfish thing, really. Because I don't think he'd like it much on his own, so I feel I ought to hang on until he goes [laughs]. But I would prefer to die first. And as I say, I always thought that I probably might. My lifespan is probably just genetically shorter than his. The other thing is, you know, thinking about [my grand]children and thinking, *Well, it would be nice to see their children.* Their future, not their children necessarily, but what they do. It would be awful to die before you know how they're settled. I've always said eighty. This is when I was going to take my pill. But as you're getting towards eighty you're thinking, *Oh, hang on a minute, I can wait and take it a little bit later.* I worry about my grandchildren and what the world's going to be like. It would be nice to see that it wasn't as bad as I thought it might be, really. That's probably the good thing—to drop down dead before you see it all. I'm never going to see what's going to happen in the future, am I?

It's the final ending. I don't see any ongoing thing, or popping up to heaven or down to hell. No, I just see it as death, like the people we used to dissect in the anatomy room were dead. They were bodies, not people. Yeah, I absolutely see it like that. It's an ending. I mean, you go in the ground and that's quite good, or you go in the fiery furnace. Pop through the door! I still don't really know what I want done with mine. I think burning, probably, because it's a bit of a fuss, the burial, isn't it? You'll be agonising now [laughs]. Oh god. I honestly don't care. It doesn't really matter. I'll never see it again and it means nothing to me at all. You can do what you like.

92.

Having grown up in a concreted new town that was as far away from the sea as you could possibly get on our little, narrow island, I always got thrilled to bits whenever we went. When I was a little girl I used to go to the beach with my granny and grandad, cos my grandad was a big fisherman. They didn't live by the sea, it used to be a big outing. They used to stick me and my brother in the back of my grandad's building van and drive us down to Winchelsea beach. We'd usually have to stop off at some point and sit on the side of the road and eat Granny's Marmite and lettuce sandwiches. She used to keep the lettuce in a Tupperware box with a little piece of coal in it to keep it crunchy [laughs]. I don't know whether that was because the little bits of coal fell off into the lettuce and made it crunchy! And so we used to do that and then head on down to Winchelsea beach and make camp by the groynes there. And Grandad'd spend the whole day fishing. He caught a little tiny shark once—which I often think about, in fact, when I'm swimming in the sea, that if that was a baby shark there might be bigger sharks out there. I used to collect loads of pebbles and make them into little houses and bits of furniture for the houses and so on.

Nowadays I usually try to look for one that's got a remarkable pattern on it. In fact, the other day I was sitting on the beach and I picked up a pebble to look at it and when I turned it over, it had this awful screaming face etched into it, just through the power of the sea. It utterly reflected my mood that day, when I'd been feeling really low, and the first stone I picked up was like looking in the mirror, basically, to my emotions. But there are lots of funny little stones as well. They might look like a little sea lion flapping his fins or his tail or look like somebody with a big nose or something. Talking of sea lions, there's a seal that comes on _____ beach every year called Trevor. Is it Trevor? He's named after the man that first spotted him, I think [laughs]. He must be passing by once a year, at a particular time, I suppose. But this year I saw him and he'd really aged since last year. He'd grown a lot of hair. He had a lockdown hairdo. Black, matted fur all over him. Another visit we had this year was a turtle. Two friends of mine, they go swimming along the sea, proper swimming with fluorescent buoys and wetsuits, and they swim across the bay every morning. And they came across this turtle and it was stranded on the beach. So they rescued it and took it to the Sea Life Centre. And it was all in the news that they'd done this turtle rescue and then it died [laughs]. So it was really awful for them. Because one minute they were heroes and the next minute they'd basically brought about the demise of this poor turtle by taking him out of his natural habitat.

I've got quite a few good skinny-dipping stories. Me and my brother went to the Zap Club in Brighton, and afterwards we were so hot because we'd been dancing about, and we just stripped off, ran down Brighton beach and jumped in the sea naked. And whilst we were in the sea, some lads came by and nicked our clothes. [My brother] got out of the sea and was legging it down the beach after them, everything dangling, shouting like some kind of crazy person. They dropped the clothes and ran, cos they were shit-scared of him. I think a shouting naked man is probably more scary, isn't it, than a shouting clothed man? It shows bravado, doesn't it, if someone's willing to chase after you without anything on!

I always wanted to come and live at the sea. That was my dream. And I've never really got over that. It makes you feel like you can see the exit. Because that's the exit from England, on the south coast, is the sea. That's how you can get away. Should you need to. If you're in IKEA you can't see the exit. You know, it's somewhere down that yellow brick road that's going round IKEA. That's not a very good feeling and that's the feeling I get when I'm in London or a big city. But when I'm living on the coast, you know that on one side of you is the exit. You just have to head south. The bit of the coast where I live, you can see the ferry going over to France, twice a day. That's very heartening to know—that you could get away if you wanted to. And actually, that makes it even more exciting when you're swimming in the sea and the ferry comes along, cos you think about your legs being underwater with the massive big ferry. That's really exhilarating, scary—which is what happens when you're in the sea or next to the sea. Like, the other day I was going for a run and I stood listening to my music up really loud, daring the sea to come up and make me wet. And obviously it did. But that felt really great, really exciting, really scary. Like letting the light in. And that's why my phone then wouldn't work. Cos the plug hole got wet.

93.

Me, I am an elderly person, as they say. Came from a rural area, went to Belfast at the end of the sixties, there began my life of believing the revolution was just gonna happen, there and then. I still believe it's gonna happen but it mightn't happen here, and it mightn't happen in my lifetime [laughs]. I went to uni, became involved in what would now be described as community activism and left-wing politics. For most of my early adult life, we used to think it would be great if we could live to forty. I remember thinking when I got to fifty, *How did I get here?* And now that I've hit seventy, I think that I definitely am one of the lucky ones. I think of the utter and appalling waste of life during our sordid sectarian squabble, aided and abetted by an establishment that thought, *Well sure, if we just keep them at each other's throats* . . . And that's being benign about their attitudes. I hate and resent that the solution to ending the violence was institutionalising sectarianism in our political life but I didn't have a better way of ending the violence, you know. That was very hard to swallow. And I think everything that has followed in terms of political behaviour has probably told the world yet again that power sharing is not necessarily a great model of sound political structures, you know [laughs].

What do I want? I want a more equal world, that's for sure. In every part of it, including this little sectarian mess hole that we have, right through to the world stage. Because if this virus hasn't underlined that reality for everybody, we're all in trouble. Inequality arises from how systems and states and nations and the world is organised, and while some years ago we might all have thought you change the capitalist system to a socialist system and everything will be hunky-dory, I think that has long evaporated. But there are a number of steps. Making sure that every child has as good a start in life as is humanly possible. Interventions to assist families, whatever their structure, to get their heads around how to manage with children and providing support to enable those kids to have the best nutrition, to have the best opportunities for eating, to have the best opportunities for socialisation, and for different experiences. That's at one end, and at the other end of the scale, you have to do something about income inequalities. Unequal societies are more unhappy than more equal societies. You work out what you think is a reasonable income distribution from top to bottom and then you say, *Yeah, we'll keep our wages on that scale.* Possibly one of the things that might evolve out of this virus, you know—because good things do come out of bad things— we might go some way in some countries to establishing a universal income, because economies have been so crushed. And that would be no comfort to those who've died and have caught the damn thing, but it would be a gain for future generations, I think.

There's a huge gap between what people think they're going to get out of protests and what they actually get. I do think, certainly at the end of the sixties, the student view was change just happens because we are on the streets demanding it [laughs]. How noble and naive were we, you know? But that's the revolution, the unfinished business of all of our hearts' desires for a better world. And in truth, the other part of that is that there is no such thing as a finished and completed revolution, because if you don't continually keep at it, you lose it. So the revolution has a bit to go [laughs]. Just a little bit, just a little bit. I don't know what difference the technological revolution makes to all of this, you know. Not being a techie person, I don't see much good of it [laughs], but that could be a bias on my part. I have no idea whether what's happening in the world of technology contributes to the revolution or the counter-revolution.

Let's talk about hope. Your life is hope, the fact that you're living is hope. The fact that we don't want to die, however inevitable it is, is hope. I mean, I think it will be hard for any future generation to make as bad a mess of the world as we have made of it. In global terms, I really do think, in the West anyway, we screwed up everything we were given. I don't say *we* as a collective, but society screwed up everything it was given and refused to learn lessons. I think future generations might be less cavalier, shall we say, about how they live and order their lives. And [the] hope is that—I don't like these words, good, bad, and all that—but that there is enough goodwill and good intentions and sound minds in the world to right a lot of the wrongs. We've gotta find a way to harness some of the social solidarity that has come through bad experiences and drive that forward into betterment of things as opposed to just preventing bad things. That would be my big hope—that we find a way to harness solidarity and cohesion and standing together to improve things that are within our grasp in whatever setting we are. That will have to be doable, you know. That will be doable, yeah.

94.

It was hardly a relationship, it was the start of a relationship.
I was challenged to ask what I was seeking. I responded
that I wanted a tantric-type relationship. Then I realised,
Gosh, I've said that, do I really know what I mean by that?
I signed up to a one-off workshop, for a week, in tantra, and
I really landed on my feet. It was an incredible experience,
so I enrolled on an eighteen-month programme. People
think that tantra's about sexuality, and yes it is, in the sense
that sexuality is so suppressed in our culture, but really
tantra is about everything in life all woven together, and
the spirituality of that. Initially there was quite a focus on
the sexuality side because it's so suppressed, but within the
eighteen-month programme, we moved on and looked at all
sorts of topics to do with spiritual growth and development.

During that time I met someone [else] and it felt like a very
different relationship to what I'd had before. And in quite
significant part it was because of how I was changing doing
these workshops. It was the most beautiful relationship I'd
ever experienced, in terms of the slowness and the quality of
connection. But I know now that I was not really bringing
all of what I was learning back into my life. And I can say
that with compassion for myself because it was a big step,
and I hadn't done a lot of work before. I wasn't embodying
everything I was learning about, but I was scribbling the notes
in my journal, you know?

That relationship that I was in, beautiful as it was, got

ended quite abruptly after about a year. It was a real shock to my system. I'd started to realise that there were things that I needed to look at in the relationship, but I was at a very early point with that and the rug was taken out from under my feet. The person concerned decided that he was attracted to someone else. And it was devastating. So last year was really hard. Really hard. Because I had to look at myself in a way that I hadn't done before. I realised for the first time in my life the impact of my childhood on the person I'd become. The parts of my childhood that I'd thought were happy I realised were not *unhappy*, but that my parents—as all parents—weren't perfect. I developed patterns and safety nets for myself that protected me as a child, that I brought into adulthood. I really started to understand some of that, but there was an awful lot of grief that I'd had to have lost that relationship in order to get all of the learning and really feel it.

I'd slipped into a twelve-step addiction recovery programme, because the person that I'd been with was doing that because he had alcohol problems in his family, because of the effect of that dysfunction. So I found a group that felt like there was some resonance there for me and it was actually a group called Sex and Love Addicts Anonymous, and I really identified with what's called love addiction. I'd spent my life up to that point looking for a partner to make me whole, and sometimes I'd been obsessed about people, men, and gone off in a fantasy in my head that I could be in a relationship, when, in reality, there was nothing happening. I found that twelve-step, the support of that group, really helpful to understanding some of these patterns. But I soon went beyond that. For example, because of my love of the outdoors, I started exploring druidry and attending ceremonies, and that felt really good. I'm still in an advanced group with my tantra work—that's evolved and become more meaningful, in the sense of embodying it more—and I looked at things like co-dependency, which is similar to love addiction.

I went through some really dark phases with it, actually, really dark spaces, and there was one point at the end of last year that I felt like I couldn't go on. And then the idea of coming back here surfaced again, and so I came here in October, just for a week, to see whether I was being pulled to come here, or whether I was trying to escape what was back home. I'd also booked to come in January for two weeks, cos I thought, *See what it's like in the winter*. And by then there was a space in the membership process, so I spoke to the members during that two weeks, and there was an attuning process, and really it felt like, *Well, if it's a no for me to come back then it's a no*, and I knew that if it was a yes that I'd come back and quit my job and rent my house. And I got the yes.

Spirituality is a flow, it's one thing leading to the next so naturally, like it was meant to be. So that's what happened [laughs]. And here I am. I came here intending—if everything works out, I'm still a trial member—that I'd be here for two or three years, that's what I said to people back in the North East when I left. And I don't know, I don't know what it will look like after this. I don't want to be as I was. I'll be me but I'll be different.

95

I used to go to speedway quite a bit when I was younger, used
to go and see Newcastle Diamonds. The smell! When I went,
the World Champion was a guy called Ivan Major. I can't
remember where he was from. He wasn't British or nowt like
that. But he had a gold-plated motorbike. It were on show
and I remember going to see that and thinking, *Wow, that's
something else.*

I left school and I worked in a back-street garage and then
worked in a main dealer, and then I got involved in the fast
fit stuff, back in the early eighties when lots of money was
being made in fast fit—fitting exhausts and tyres and all that
sort of stuff. It was all impact guns that you used, everything
was an impact gun and quite often it would be like a nut and
bolt, so you've got a spanner on one and then a gun on the
other, and you end up doing both hands. So that's what I got
into and then your body just rebels. I've got—erm, what's it
called?—in my wrists and hands. Repetitive strain. I'm at the
stage now where if I get a tie, I've got one attempt to get me
tie fastened cos I can't hold it the second time if I don't get it
right. If I do a crappy knot I just gotta live with it! I like the
half-Windsor and I used to be able to do them nae problem.
I got meself a good one and kept it. I've had the same knot
for, I would say, four funerals! Four funerals and a wedding
[laughs].

I've got the best job in the world. I absolutely love my job,
apart from I have to stop away, on average a couple of times

a week. I'm in training and development. I work for a tyre wholesaler and we go out and we do product knowledge and a bit of sales training for independent garages. The public treat tyre fitters like second-class citizens. I don't know many tyre fitters who aspired to be that when they left school, but then they're store people, they're ordering stock, they're using computers, they're answering phones, they're dealing with customers, they're doing a hell of a lot apart from just fit tyres. But everybody looks down on them.

I say it to them: *People go on about nurses and how they save lives and all this sort of stuff. You can save lives by giving people the right advice.* Everybody assumes that when I turn up I'm gonna teach 'em how to rip somebody off. It's the total opposite. It's about keeping your customers safe and giving the best advice. I get to speak to loads of people and there's very few that I met that I divn't like. Would you believe it? I've been doing this for six years, I've met thousands of people and I can probably count on one hand the number of people that I didn't get on with. Because I've got something in common with most of them. There's nearly always a connection somewhere. I talk on their level. I don't like dealing with the management side of it so much. I like dealing with the blue-collar workers, cos that's what I am. I'm a blue-collar worker, really. So I can talk their language—and if they like to swear, so much the better [laughs].

It actually annoys me quite a bit how ignorant some people are. I mean, I'm not gonna tell you who I work for, but I work for a big company who's got, I think, about eighteen hundred employees, something like that. They've got managers and area managers and sales managers who've done all the courses and can talk the talk and they can't walk the walk. They keep people in the dark—they're mushroom managers, basically. They keep you in the dark and feed you shit. They don't even know what motivates their staff and they're not even interested in knowing what motivates their staff. They all think people are motivated by money and they're not. I don't know very many people who are. You need money to live. But you're doing what you do because you enjoy doing it, yeah? You've got all these managers out there who never speak to their staff unless it's to give them a bollocking or something like that. They're just, *Do this, do that*. They treat their staff like shit.

Funnily enough, I met a guy, did some training with him, big bloke from the other side of Birmingham, absolutely massive, and I did a communication course with him, and we were talking about communicating with your staff and all this, that and t'other. And then a couple of days later one of his guys was late in and he actually phones us up, and he went, *Normally I woulda just bollocked him but,* he says, *I remembered what you said, so I went along and had a quiet word, a chat with him and said, y'know, 'Is everything okay?'* And it turned out that he'd split up with his girlfriend and he'd had to go and live with his mother, miles away. And he says, *Now I've got that but normally I woulda just bollocked him.* And I went, *Happy days! You've seen the light! You've seen the light!!*

96.

The estate I live on it was sort of half council and half private and we was the council side. We were the rough-and-readies, just herberts, little street herberts, really. We didn't mix with the other lot. Not that we were poor, we were just on the poor side of the tracks. We was out stealing bikes and just being arseholes really. The older kids were doing it, you just went with it. A bit of peer pressure, I suppose. Got caught a few times, went to court, youth court. Got caught in a car. I wasn't even driving it. I was just a passenger. They still throw the book at you. I tried to get out of it. I think it was my solicitor who said, *Tell them you're joining the army, that'll keep you out of borstal.* I said I was joining the army to keep out of borstal and it just happens one of the judges was a cadet leader and he goes, *Well, I'll keep an eye on you. I want you to bring your papers to me next week.* You try to get out of something, you try to blag it, and it shot me in the foot. I thought, *I'll give it a whirl.* And signed up. Again, had no intention of turning up. Turned up. Loved it. Absolutely loved it.

Yeah, Northern Ireland, Bosnia. Then more recently, I left and I got called up as a reservist in 2003. Went out to Iraq in 2003 as a reservist, and I went to Afghanistan in 2006. I didn't know they could do it. Letter come through my door and I thought it was a joke: *Yeah, whatever.* I called them up and they went, *Nah, you need to go to Nottingham.* They weren't recruiting properly. They were short of people. They give you

206

a rail ticket one way. It's called a travel warrant. They said, *If you don't wanna go, you don't have to go.* They called up five hundred people and they rejected roughly half. And then as it goes on, they rejected more and more. Some woman turned up, she had two kids, she was told she had to go and she said, *Well, who's gonna look after these? I'm a single parent.* One bloke turned up, one leg. Lost his leg in a motorcycle accident. There was a bloke had been called up, he was eighty-six years old, he was a veteran of Korea, and he got called up by mistake. He was in the newspapers and everything. He was in my unit! He was game! He wanted to go! He said, *I'll do it!* We had one bloke, he was about twenty-seven stone.

I was in Iraq for eight months. It was quite a long tour, that. Especially as someone that's a civilian now. You know, I been out fifteen years! Afghanistan, I was only out there for six weeks. I got hit with a bit of shrapnel, on an IED. Yeah, driving a lorry. It's a roll-on roll-off, a bit like a Biffa bin lorry, but a military one. It's soft skinned, it's a fibreglass body, so when the bomb went off, the vehicle in front of us, it shattered everything. They welded these plates in, a bit sort of World War Two-ish really. We never had armoured vehicles. They have now. Everything's armoured out there. But when I was there it was all soft-skinned stuff. Truck I was in, the cab was fibreglass. It's got a bit of protection but it's not really meant for driving over bombs or driving into firefights and things. The bullets just go through it. They put these two metal plates in for a bit of protection. But we called it the Coffin [laughs].

They'd packed [the IED] with ball bearings, glass, anything else they can get in there—stones, anything. It just came and shattered the whole lorry really. It was a shell, this one was, they said, an old Russian artillery shell. They just put a detonator wire on it and explode it. It just erupts. I remember it going really dark really quickly and then really light again, that's all I remember. That was basically the earth and mud shooting up in the air. It was instant, like lights on, lights off. It was so quick. I didn't even realise I was hit. You know, the windscreen had gone, half the cab had been shot off. Bloke next to me, he was hurt worse. Didn't know him. It was only really when my boot was filling up with blood and I went, *What's going on there?*—then I realised. Went down, felt it. It's come straight through the side of the truck.

It's not too bad. Bit of metal stuck in there. Dunno what it was. They got it out. No, no one was killed. We were lucky. We were so lucky. The vehicle in front, they were all a lot worse off than I was. One amputee, he lost a couple of legs. One of them got a head wound. I was in hospital in Bastion and then Medivacced out, sent home. That was it. Nah! Nah! No. Nah, nah, they pay you your wages and as soon as you leave that's it. *You're a reservist. See you later. Bye, thanks!*

97

I sit with people who are dying.

I get these calls out of the blue, and I don't know the people at all, and I respond to every single one, wherever they are, and for me it's an honour. And if I can make someone peaceful in their last moments, if I can make their family peaceful in their last moments, that for me feels very humbling. It's a massive responsibility, but I feel when I've left that I've done something good. I'll get a call to sit with someone because they've asked somebody to come who's a medium and who's been recommended. What very often happens, when a person is in the last couple weeks of their life, they start to see people in their room that they love who have gone before. It's incredibly common, lots and lots of nurses will tell you about the same thing. It's a very peaceful feeling for me because I know they're gonna be alright. But I can also feel the excitement building in the room with other people who are coming to get them. Some people I've seen when they leave their body, at the actual point of their passing. My friend's mum, I was sat with her for hours, and I suddenly felt the room become very active, almost like electricity. And I said to her, *You better say what you wanna say, cos it's gonna happen any minute now.* So she did. And I said, *Look at her head,* and as we looked at her head, all these tiny, tiny silver sparks were coming out above her head. It was the most incredible thing. The nurse came in and checked her, and she'd gone. Another lady I saw leave as vapour, she seemed to go from her solar plexus, and just come out as vapour, energy, really. If you ever see a deceased person, you can tell the personality is gone, whoever they were has gone, just left the vehicle.

Sometimes it's a room full of people. One [example] was a lady who asked me to go up and see her dad. He was passing with cancer of the stomach, and I was sat in his room, and he's in that very heavy medicated state, and his daughter's sat opposite me, and we're just chatting. I can always feel when people are arriving. This man walked in behind her with a huge tummy, absolutely enormous tummy, and he said, *I'm his brother*, and he says, *I went with a heart attack.* I said, *Did you have an uncle who had a really big tummy?* And she said, *Oh my god, yeah, it was huge.* Then a little boy came in, and he said, *I'm his brother as well*, and he said, *I drowned when I was eight.* And I said to her, *Did your dad have a brother who drowned when he was eight?* She goes, *Oh god, yeah. He drowned in the stream by what is now Morrisons.* Then a man came in who only had one leg, and he had a Jack Russell with him. So he comes in and he said he was his friend and they used to meet once a week on the wall at the Post Office to get their pension and have a fag and a chat. And she was absolutely floored because he'd died a fortnight before, and her dad didn't know yet. So he comes in as well. Then her mum came in. She stood at the end of the bed, looking at him, and he's looking back at her, and then these tears just start to go down here. I could tell they were happy tears, and I'm reassuring him all the time that he's seeing these people and she's stood at the end of the bed. I asked her, *I know you're gathering because you're gonna take him. When is it that you're gonna take him?* That was the following day, and what was really nice about it, it gave them time to get all the family up there to say goodbye. Everybody came in, saw him, said goodbye, and he passed the next day, at the time his wife said. [His daughter] says how peaceful he was, because now he knew it was real. All his life he'd fought against it, and now at the very end of his life, it was real, and all the people he'd loved had come to get him. So that makes me feel incredible.

People fear death. I get that, because you don't want to leave everything you know and family and all the rest of it. But I think more, they fear how they're gonna go. They always seem to send the person you loved the most, because they know you will go with them without question, because you're so thrilled to see them. And when people see them, they may not have been clairvoyant in their lives at all, but when they see them, they see them as clearly as I do. Because they're leaving, because part of them is already leaving, because they've partly excarnated, they can then see the spirit person. So they know it's their mum or son or I don't know. So yeah, it is incredible.

98.

A load of the time, when people are considering form in relation to music, they talk about it as the antithesis of chaos. From my position, the chaos just doesn't exist. The chaos is an inability to recognise a form that's not apparent at the beginning. For me, if you can see the shape or not see the shape, there's no real difference. Cos the shape's still gonna be there. That was one of the breakthroughs in my career in terms of the ability to relax about my misgivings—you know, about the things that I didn't know. Or the elements of complexity that I just didn't have the time or the inclination to try to beat into myself. If you can hear something and you play it and it is truly what you want to express with the others that are around you, then that is it. That's it. Full stop. Whether you understand the form and the structure of that on a technical level or on an intuitive level is neither here nor there.

And, you know, if you wanna go back to more nefarious usages of that same type of thinking, it's the same basic way of seeing that is, essentially, the colonial encounter— of seeing an Other and saying what the Other is doing. I've been thinking a lot about civilisation versus savagery. Especially at this juncture, where it looks like what we think of as being the civilising mission of the West is actually, in a broad schema, the thing that's [lead]ing the planet to destruction. The original mercenaries/adventurers who went over from the time of Columbus, when they would first go over to the Americas or to Africa—they saw native people doing what they were doing and said, *They are doing nothing. What they're doing has no form and it has no consequence as far as we see consequence. Therefore, it must be chaos and it must be formless. And we're going to show them what the Truth and the Light is, according to Christianity*—which was a part of the same thing. If you think of that in terms of an imposed form on what was assumed to be chaos—but wasn't actually chaos, it was just the unknown—then the whole thing kind of makes sense.

What is chaos? We use the word as the antithesis of form and structure. Or it's just things happening randomly. But that is actually the antithesis of spirituality. My spirituality assumes some form of cosmology, which means that everything does have a structure, but within a scheme that's beyond our comprehension. It doesn't mean that you believe, necessarily, in the form of spirituality professed by organised groups. Essentially, it's cause and effect. We just see a bunch of the effects and go, *Well, these things came out of nowhere!* You know, *For no reason!* And for me that really doesn't make sense. Even if you're looking at it scientifically, that really doesn't make any sense. Everything has causes, but the causes might be hidden. Or forgotten.

It's like this society—it's got an interest in making us think that things aren't precarious, that as society progresses things are becoming more stable. It goes back to that idea of progress, or the idea of evolution—the idea that things are progressing on an upwards trajectory for everyone. And this is why, for instance, the storming of the Capitol building was so shocking to everyone. But it shouldn't be shocking at all. It's obvious that something like that could and would happen at some point. Because Americans are buck wild and they've always been buck wild. It's a nation of cowboys, you know, with their guns that they proudly lobby for. This goes back to the idea of progress—because America is in the business of selling. It's a salesman state and what they sell is hope and dreams. What is a dream? A dream is a projection of reality that is not true. America is in the business of projecting dreams, and that dream is that from the original sin—which is taking a bunch of land from other people—[comes] progress: they weren't doing anything with the land before they came and by utilising the land in the way that American Europeans have, that is progressing civilisation and therefore the world. But if you forget that idea of progress, then things can actually go backwards. And actually, if you look at the African ontological system of the circle, things don't go forward in a linear fashion, things come around and there will be a constant revolving of civilisation and barbarity. It's two sides of a coin that is constantly revolving.

Ideas are cheap. Ideas come fast, you know. Ideas are everywhere. There's innumerable ideas. The thing is not about getting ideas. The thing is actually *not* getting ideas. It's actually stilling the mind so you are not bombarded with lots and lots of different impulses to think about different things. Then what is important kind of cuts down the middle. And I think when I'm playing, when everything is working,

I'm not thinking about anything, all I'm doing is listening to others and how what I'm doing relates to the whole.

99

Right now I want chocolate because I'm on a new diet with my PT [personal trainer] and I have to count my macros and I have to decide whether I want to treat myself and cook my vegetables with butter or whether I wanna have chocolate. So that's what I want right now.

More seriously, a lot of the work I do is around increasing awareness and education around issues that trans people face in the world. And the direction I wanted to take it in was specifically through the lens of healthcare and sport. The current healthcare pathway is that you can see a doctor, you see a specialist, and if the specialists say you're all good to go, you can then get access to hormones and surgeries— wonderful. However, the waiting times are between twelve to sixteen months to see a specialist. All I want in the world is for those waiting times to actually be in line with the NHS guidelines, which is like fourteen weeks, instead of fourteen months. And for people to have healthy, happy coping mechanisms for dealing with things like gender dysphoria and all the other wonderfulness that comes with being trans, that isn't just, *Wait a year or two and if you're still alive we're gonna inject you with a bunch of stuff.* I got involved with the sport route because it was one of the few ways I could find which is a way of improving your mental health, improving your physical health, and changing your physical appearance in a way that is sustainable and isn't relying on external medication. And it's also pretty accessible and available to most people.

I want you to be happy in this environment, I want you to walk into a gym, not have an anxiety attack, and realise how you can make yourself happier and change your body to fit whatever aesthetic you want. Everyone has this impression of gym facilities that it's just a bunch of steroided-out guys whose necks are bigger than me, and it's just horrible. And to be fair, some gyms are like that, and that's really toxic, and I don't like it. But also at the other end of the spectrum, you can have small community gyms that are literally just a bunch of old ladies with tiny little weights, just trying to keep moving and being happy and the person there is playing swing music from the fifties, and that's what works for them. Physical activity and exercise take different forms for a bunch of different people. If you're gonna be a good PT, it's working out what motivates and what inspires your client. I had a guy that I was training with a little while ago. He's a bit of a bigger guy, he's also a trans guy, and he was really self-conscious in a gym facility. I did an entire session with him where we basically pretended to be pirates. Cos it was funny. He's a massive musical nerd, so we were singing sea shanties. It made him happy and made him forget he was in a gym.

Something that I think a lot of trans people experience when they initially come out and are starting to transition is you have this loss of bodily autonomy. There's this big conception—you're born in the wrong body. It's a bit of a fallacy. That means that if you take my brain out, or my consciousness out, and put it in a different body, I'd feel okay?

No, this is the only thing I'm born with. And if you don't feel comfortable in your own skin, it has a massive impact on your mental health. At one end of it, you might not even be able to recognise your own reflection, you feel so uncomfortable that you don't know what else to do. Whereas something as simple as exercise, even if you remove the trans element from it entirely, it's good for your mental health, it will produce your serotonin, and then on top of that, you can almost dictate how your physical appearance looks. If I wanna look absolutely massive, I can be absolutely massive, I just have to eat a ton of food and lift these weights. If I wanna get really slim, I eat these foods, I lift these weights. If I wanna look like an upside-down triangle, I can do that! And it all just depends on the person, and as long as you've got a culture of information around you, you can do whatever you like.

Trans people are human. We just wanna be happy and find ways of making [ourselves] happy and comfortable in our own bodies, whatever form that takes. What I want is for people to recognise the potential in different activities, realise that working out is not just one very specific thing in one specific style, and you have to spend a ton of money on gym clothes and all this rubbish. It's what works for you. If you wanna go rock climbing, go rock climbing. Don't let anything stop you.

100.

I learnt a lot of harsh lessons when I went through my divorce. One of them was that, ultimately, a woman is expected to sacrifice and if we don't sacrifice, then the people around us suffer. And I don't feel that men are under that obligation. For a long while, I was a single parent with a young child. I had to keep a roof over her head, I had to have a job that worked around her school holidays and her school timings. I needed to heal, she needed to heal as well. So I work in schools, and I'm not a teacher, and I get paid a shitty wage, to be honest, even though I'm overqualified for the position, because it works well around my life. I think that men aren't expected to make as many sacrifices as women are, and that's been a bitter, unlikeable pill. This is across all faith groups and races, all across. I see it the same with my white friends, my Black friends, my Asian friends, the situations are roughly the same, where the women are the ones making the sacrifices to make the household work and run.

One of the important things I've been trying to teach [my daughter] is—and maybe this is my own personal baggage—is to like herself, and to be proud of who she is. So she's an Asian, she's Muslim, she's a girl—she's got a lot of things working against her in British society. I wasn't comfortable with who I am, growing up. I don't think I was at all. I resented being a Pakistani. I want her to like who she is. I guess I want her to know who she is and what she is and where she comes from and our place within this society. Cos quite honestly, I am made to feel that I don't belong here. Going forward, I don't believe that she won't be made to feel that. There's always positives and negatives with each identity we choose for ourselves and I don't want to put an identity on her. If she chooses to define herself by those parameters that's great. But society will always define her by those parameters, I think, as it will me. I'm a third-generation Pakistani, my grandparents were the first to come over, and yet we've never been looked at by anybody else and been told, *Well, you're English*, even though I'm English through and through. My daughter's born here, and no matter how many generations go on, as long as she continues to marry somebody of some melanated skin tone, she'll be, for want of a better term, a *P__i*, right?

I've been to Pakistan twice in my whole entire life, and I'm thirty-five now, thirty-six. Here, I was told, *Oh, you're Pakistani, you're Pakistani*. I had a few issues at secondary school with bullying and stuff, and it centred around me being Pakistani. The first time I went over to Pakistan, I was the British girl, the English girl. So you've got this dissonance within you where you're like, *Where do I fit? Where do I belong and who am I?* And I guess that's where my faith played a big part, because I maybe began to define myself through that. And maybe my daughter will be blessed not to go through these identity issues, but I don't see that things are necessarily going to change any time soon. It's amazing how English we are without realising it, because we're constantly told, *You're not English*. Well, actually I love queueing, if there's not a proper queue I get really annoyed! It's a whole host of things that we have come to like and get used to—bureaucracy and all the rest of it, the way that the systems work—and those are things that in my mind make me quite English. I'm not Welsh, I'm not Scottish, I'm not Irish. I'm English, I've been raised here.

I have lived, through choice, quite a conservative lifestyle, especially when I was younger. I wore niqab—the face cover, veil—for about four years in my early twenties. This was against the choice of my family, my family were not happy with it, nobody was pushing me to do it, these were all personal choices on my own spiritual path. The media often likes to portray people like myself as having such stringent boundaries that we are not forthcoming to change or different opinions and different views. I'm not like that at all. I like learning from people, and I like sharing in other people's experiences. I like people who are different to me, because I like to learn from them. If you're the same as me there's no room for growth. But then, see, when it comes to food, I don't like that. I don't want my boundaries pushed when it comes to food!

101.

I'm standing upstage right and I have to imagine myself
running towards me, entering my body and sending me
forward. And at the same time, I'm dragging the space with
me and I'm inviting being seen, choosing to surrender the
pattern of facing a single direction, whilst in the lab. It's crazy,
crazy fucking instructions that make no sense, that you're
grappling with and you're doing. And I did. And this solo was
always twenty-eight minutes and thirty seconds or twenty-
eight minutes and fifty-two seconds, even though it was in
silence. Oh hi, darling! Sorry, it's my husband back. And at
a certain point I have to sing in a fake voice and I sing in the
fake voice in a fake language backwards—like a beautiful
song. Ooh, sorry, he's holding up two sandwiches. Oh, why
don't we share half and half? We're sharing half and half.
The score is so dense and the thinking of the doing of it is
very dense, it sends you into a semi-trance state, I would say.
During the performance of it. Not in a weirdy-woo way. I'm
still really present with the audience, but it was a big shift.
I can remember the experience of it like it was last week. At
one point I was slowly moving away from the audience, from
downstage to upstage, and I could feel heat billowing out of
my T-shirt like that. And there's this bit as well when you
talk, you have to speak in an ancient voice. And it was like *The
Exorcist*. It was like some old bloke suddenly came out.

   I started dancing really late, when I was fourteen. I took
it as an extra GCSE. I thought, *Oh, I want an extra one.*

So rather than doing cross-country I'll do dance [laughs].
The local animateur for O_____ Council came and said, *I've
got dance classes and they're free*, and I'm like, *I'm there!*
Cos basically I always wanted to go to dance classes but
my parents were too poor to send me. I was from a quite
working-class, immigrant, poor background. So I was right
there and I just thought, *This is my tribe*. I don't know how I
found out about stuff but I would get the bus to Manchester
and go to the avant-garde theatre to watch weird shit, and to
me this was like the coolest thing I'd ever encountered. I was
like, *This is for me*. I hadn't had a lot of training in my body
so I was a little bit out of control, but I had tons of energy.
And the thing I could do really well, right from the start, was
I could see a sequence of movement once and recall it. I was
like Rain Man, you know. I could just see that thing and I'd
go, *Yeah, got it*. And I could just do it. I don't know how. I
could see this movement map out for me.

People often think thinking is words, you know, words
appearing in your mind. That's what thoughts are. But
actually, look at any one-year-old, and just cos they can't
speak doesn't mean they're not thinking. You can see their
brain firing in all sorts of directions. They're learning and
working it out. There's this really gorgeous dance scholar
who says, rather than saying that children are pre-linguistic
we have to think of ourselves as post-kinetic. We lose what
[we] started with, right? The body isn't like a car for my
brain but the whole lot is brain. Movement is a cognitive
activity. For you to know what a sunset looks like, you don't

have to put it into words. You can recall that, can't you?
You might feel it down the back of your neck or you might
feel it, I don't know, in your chest or something. It's about
equalising language, cos I think there is often a hierarchy
where words are seen as more important than stuff like
dancing. We have to open up our experience in order to,
I think, tap into a richer understanding of our world and
ourselves and each other.

[The choreographer] said, *I'm not interested in what you
do. I'm interested in seeing you in the act of perception,
in the act of perceiving. The dance is not the movement.* I
thought, *This is for me.* It was like being fourteen again.
It was quite a profound experience because all of a sudden
I couldn't really draw upon any kind of choreographic
information I'd had up until that point. It kind of stripped
that away. So what was left, I felt, was my movement identity.
For the first time in my career, I felt I was dancing me.

102.

I used to be a person that wanted a lot of things. If I think back to my youth, my pre-pubescent youth was about wanting [to be] living in better conditions, it was about wanting to be safe. I grew up really poor so I wanted very bread-and-butter things as a child. My wife is a little bit younger than me, she's grown up very comfortably, very privileged. She never needed or wanted anything. She cannot grasp the appreciation for basic stuff, because she's never spent a winter sleeping in her coat as a child. I grew up in an apartment building where we had no central heating, there was no radiators on the wall, the walls and floors were concrete, we had no double glazing. In winter if you breathed, you'd see the fog inside of the room from your breath.

I think my adolescence and my formative years made me want *everything*. I wanted to be respected, I wanted to be feared, I wanted to be wealthy. I wanted all of the hyper-masculine, toxic fuckery that men from London of a certain era wanted: leather jackets, fast cars, sexy girlfriends, gold chains, all of that. BMWs and Avirex jackets and hundred-pound trainers and all of this other bullshit that actually you don't really need, but you just really fucking want. Capital letters *WANT*, yeah? By the time I was twenty-three, all of the things that I '*wanted*' I had achieved. But all of that wanting definitely had a price, and the price attached to all of that wanting and [the] achieving of all that wanting was my relationships with people were bad, and my lifestyle was bad.

The price of wanting so much, all at once, was quite heavy. But I've emerged the other side of my thirties not wanting too much at all, really. I'm very much in a space where, you know, if you want it, I've got it, if you've got it, I've had it. I'm in that space. So there's not much to achieve in wanting, and my needs are very simple.

Wanting is normal. And there are some people who are told that they're not allowed to want—they're not allowed to want better for themselves, they're not allowed to want better things, they're not allowed to enjoy luxury because of their circumstance. I was in a multi-agency gang meeting with lots of different people—the police, mental health workers, the emergency services, everybody involved in this crisis meeting about the gang situation in this city. And the consultant that was working there, he was wearing a TAG Heuer watch, he had a great pair of handmade shoes on, great suit, he had a new Volvo parked outside, you could guarantee that he goes on holiday to nice places with his family or his significant others or whatever. But his perspective was, *These young gang members are committing serious crime just because they want stuff that's not important, just because they want to go to Selfridges and buy expensive clothes, or just because they want to have a nice car.* Actually they just want the same shit that he wants. That he's already got. Everybody wants the same shit in that kind of weird, *wanting*, capitalist buy-in kinda way. These supervillains that this guy was consulting about—what they want, it's the same stuff that he wants and has. But because they are from low-income parts of the city and are uneducated and unemployed, they're not allowed to want the same shit that he's got.

I am sure that my basic wants and needs are the same as everybody else's on Earth. I'm sure that everybody else feels the same, everybody wants the same thing. We know money doesn't buy happiness, we know people confuse respect with fear, we know that just because you're feared, you're not safe. Which is all rhetorical stuff that's in the universe, circling Instagram as a meme somewhere. But it's just really true. It's just really true. We wanna be safe, we wanna be secure, and we do wanna be respected, by each other. I need to feel safe and secure, I need to be able to provide for my family, I need to be able to survive in the world. Not survive, actually—to thrive. To thrive and be productive and successful in a world that's not designed for me to do that. I'm not supposed to be here. I'm not supposed to be here now, talking to you about this with this perspective. I'm supposed to either be still wrapped up in the wanting things, or chewed up and spat out of the other end of that wanting phase.

So that's where I'm at.

103

It was a very toxic experience. People had made their minds up based on, I think, a lot of lies. I mean, the attitude to people on the doors—getting followed around by people, getting really angry assaults from some people that I actually personally knew and had helped with various projects. The whole part that social media played in that—people getting so radicalised by what they'd be reading online and believing. I don't know where else it would be coming from, that they would be attacking simple facts about what was actually going on. It was producing quite an aggressive response. So yeah, it definitely took me quite a while to get over that. And before Covid hit, trying to motivate myself. It was quite difficult to make myself go back out again. It was like, *Oh god, I just don't want to do it again.* And when it all got called off, I really didn't mind that much. I just don't think I could do it again.

And then we had lockdown, and yes it was scary, but we had the period that really did feel like everybody put lots of differences aside, whether they were political party differences or whether they were, you know, Brexit differences. None of that mattered for a while, and we all pulled together and we all tried to protect people and save as many lives as was possible. So it was really, really busy, yeah, really, really busy, but it did feel like we were all in it together. You hear these phrases being used as a political slogan a lot, but it did actually feel like that. The community really stepped up, nearly three hundred people volunteered to help out those who were vulnerable and pretty much everybody who was on furlough did something if they were able, so it was quite a good time.

Now again we're seeing a lot of culture wars—like you've got the people who won't wear masks, and everybody wants to claim that they've got a medical condition that means that they can't wear a mask—you know, *I can't wear a mask because I've got asthma.* So that started to pick up. And then you got a lot of people who don't wanna take the vaccine, and a lot of misinformation going around. The problem is a lie's halfway around the world before the truth's got its boots on. Especially [with] Facebook, you're connected in with the people you know and trust the most—you've connected in with your friends and family. Everybody that I know now has got at least one person in their social circle that really believes in QAnon, for example—that there is this anonymous deep-state voice that's telling people that the Democrats in America are Satan-worshipping paedophiles. I mean, just saying that out loud, how would anybody believe that? But people do, and it triggers a lot of fear and anger and worry and makes them go and preach to everybody else, and then it starts to infect whole groups of people. Same with the anti-vaxxing stuff, same with the anti-masking stuff. I've got a lot of people in my social circle who are getting crazy ideas about vaccines because of the subgroups that they're in. There's a whole environmental subgroup that doesn't like vaccinations, so some alternative therapy people seem to be affected a lot. Actually some people that I know went on the anti-lockdown march, so were marching side by side with white-supremacist far-right people, and this is an issue that's brought those kind of groups together, which is really worrying. I think what people are saying is, *I'm scared of this thing that I don't understand.* What people don't realise is that these people—who's the lizard man?— actually make a lot of money out of conspiracy theories. There's a number of figures who make a very nice living out of pushing conspiracy theories, and then the platforms that they push them on—Facebook, YouTube, etcetera—also make a lot of advertising revenue out of these people with big followings. So this is how this stuff gets out, and then it gets into people's Facebooks. And people tend to believe it because the person who's posting it is their friend or their family member. Apparently grandmas are the biggest pushers of QAnon conspiracy theories in the UK at the minute. It's your grandma who's had to tackle social media in order to talk to her grandkids during lockdown. So yeah, I think social media's like the coronavirus but for misinformation. And people, it seems, will believe any old rubbish. I don't know what you'd do about that.

104.

You'll Google it and immediately find some terrifying stuff saying it's a cult, but it isn't, I promise. It's like any of these things, there's some people it attracts that are loonies, but hopefully I'm not one of them.

Nichiren was this thirteenth-century monk in Japan who studied everything, and he settled upon the Lotus Sutra, which is the penultimate sutra that the original Buddha taught. Although it's a great big, poetic, scrambling mess of metaphors, it's essentially saying that we all have Buddhahood, all nature is Buddhahood, and what that means is that basically you have the potential for enlightenment, right now, as you are. You need to work on it a bit but you don't have to shave your head and change your name and go vegan and live on a mountain. Right now, here in life, is everything we need to transform whatever's happening into a state of enlightenment. The lotus flower grows in mud, it grows in the shit, and it flowers and fruits. None of us can avoid suffering. We're all gonna get old and die, and lose people we love, and that's just how it is. But it's essentially saying that we have the potential to reveal a state of profound happiness with just being alive. It's there, at all times, you can access it.

This is something that I kind of always knew. You get a glimpse of [it] on drugs, right? I remember once I was on the 38 bus, it was just some random Tuesday morning, and I looked at everybody and had one of those amazing moments where it feels like you're coming up on E or something, where I just thought, *We're all connected, and I love you all, and I wish you well.* You can have those moments unbidden, and they're wonderful. I had those moments as a child as well. I remember vividly looking at the sea and thinking, *I've always been here. There's something profoundly bigger than me that I'm part of.* I don't wanna get up on the pulpit, it's really important to respect that everybody believes other stuff. This isn't necessarily something which I want to go round spouting off about too often, because it really sticks in my craw when people get evangelical about stuff. But it has been really transformative and certainly helped with having a kid like _____. Basically, from the get-go, he has been somebody who, his default position is *No*, and he sort of lives to oppose and argue and test, just dance on my last nerve. I mean, I can sort of laugh about it now, but there have been times when I think I really would have been in a very dark place, and I was in a dark place, but I was more able to understand that the dark places we go to are our ways of finding light. That sounds a bit hokey but it's true.

I'd never suffered from anxiety like I did when I was pregnant. It's crazy cos we'd been trying for a kid for seven years, so you'd think I'd be cock-a-hoop that we got pregnant naturally, but actually by the time I got pregnant we'd sort of given up and moved on, and we were quite happy. We were looking forward to being those smug middle-aged people that go travelling all the time and have an amazing time. Initially I thought I would have a miscarriage because I'd had one before, and then I didn't, I went past that danger period. And then it started to actually hit me: *Oh my god, I'm gonna actually have to bring up a human being, and be everything to them for the first bit, and then also try and guide them through life.* I'm sort of vocalising it all, it wasn't that clear, it was just like I physically had a profound stress reaction to it. I literally couldn't breathe—and I use the word *literally* correctly. I mean, I was struggling, I was gasping for air quite a lot. I had a friend who was doing this practice, this chanting, and she said that it had really helped with her anxiety. I started really gently trying to do some every morning, and I did feel calmer and more optimistic afterwards. Just accepting that I am quite a nervous person but that it's gonna be okay. I began to trust myself and think, *I will undoubtedly fuck him up in some way because that's just what parents do. But it'll be okay.*

105

When you become a wrestler, when you learn to wrestle,
you're unlearning so much of what your body has learnt as a
normal human being [laughs] who doesn't throw themselves
around—particularly if you're a woman. I had to re-form
my entire body to become a wrestler, is how I see it. I'm a
woman, I was born female, I'm female-assigned at birth. I had
a normal-ish upbringing of being a girl. So I didn't play-fight.
I didn't do any sport that would have been classed as contact
sport. You're always told to be quiet, sit still, don't sit with
your legs wide open. You know, try and be dainty and petite. I
was never those things. I was always clumsy and embarrassed
by myself. I don't think boys have that same problem. I
think they have other things—that they can't be feminine
or gentle or warm or caring, that's beaten out of them. But
I also think that they have the freedom to take up space
and make noise. So when you become an adult, if you're a
woman, the relationship you have with the body in the way
that you move and the way that you express yourself, even if
it's things like absolute fucking anger—it's repressed by you
having to fit into this form. It's muscle memory. It's taught
and it's learnt. And it's hard to forget.

When you become a wrestler you have to unlearn all of
that. So, for example, you have to learn to throw yourself
backwards on to the floor hard enough that it makes noise and
it looks like someone's kicked you in the stomach. It's called
bumping. It's one of the first lessons you learn. We always say

it's the sign if you're gonna be a wrestler or not. Because either you like bumping and you're like, *Oh my god, I just made this noise! How cool is that?!* Or you're like, *That hurt so much, I never want to do it again.* Everything you've learnt is telling you, *Do not fall over backwards! Do not put your hands up!* Whereas if you're a wrestler, you have to throw your hands back, tuck your chin, and literally give it everything you've got. So you have to unlearn one of your most basic instincts, which is what to do when you're in danger. And then, once you've broken down that instinct, you learn how to build it up again so it looks more effective, more neat. You know, it makes a bigger sound when you throw yourself on the floor. Or you learn to throw yourself on the floor and then do a backward somersault, for example. That's the form that you're learning as a wrestler. It goes from breaking down everything you know to then building it back up again in a way that is elegant and controlled—and believable, most of all. And that's just one example. It goes from everything—from the way that you stand when you look like you're about to have a fight, or the way that you walk or run across the ring. You know, you start off and you're just like a person running for the bus. And then over years and months and months and weeks and years of practice, of having to do exactly the same thing—hours and hours every day of running the ropes—you start to look like a beautiful swan, like a strong person smashing into ropes and impressing everyone in the audience.

So in some ways we re-form ourselves, wrestlers. We take this person we are in the normal world and go, not necessarily, *This person isn't good enough,* but there's something deep inside you that wants to literally change every aspect of that into an alter ego. That's how I feel about it, anyway. You know, when I get into my wrestling character, when I have a match, I physically step out of my body and everything that makes me me—the way that I walk, the way that I hold myself, I have to replace it with my character. Though as I watch the videos back, I'll be looking really amazing and then there'll be a sudden moment where I clearly forget what I'm doing, and my body just reverts back to normal. I look like I'm waiting for a bus or about to be hit in the face by some random person. I no longer look like, you know, a disgusting frog woman, for example.

106

The bald head is pretty similar to a skull. You might say it's a *memento mori*. An awareness of the skeleton is something that is always quite difficult to stomach. When you think about it in an objective way, what we are is this collection of inanimate things made animate by their connections and the signals sent in between all the parts of them. It's pretty dehumanising to think of our self in pieces. But that is what we are. We're an assemblage of cells.

The first time that anyone ever commented on my hairline was when I was seventeen. Me and a couple of school friends went down to London to go and watch a gig. We were there for two nights so we did lots of very childish, touristy things. For example, we went to Portobello Road, which was somewhere I'd wanted to go because as a child my sister had loved *Bedknobs and Broomsticks*—there was a period of a couple of years where she watched that film maybe not every week but certainly at least twice a month. There's an extended musical number set in Portobello Road, which enticed me to West London, I think. My friend took a picture of me by the Portobello Road street sign. It was the first digital camera I'd owned, it had a tiny little screen on the back to display the picture, and when we looked at it, my friends both went, *Woah, never realised how high your hairline was! Are you already going bald?* At the time I probably just brushed it off as teasing, playing around. Verbal horseplay. But in my early twenties my hairline started going back more and more and then pretty soon whenever I sat down there'd be hair everywhere.

I had a family member, married to one of my aunts, who visibly wore a wig the whole time that me and my sister were growing up. And it was something we always used to, I suppose, laugh at but also not really understand. And I think seeing that kind of misplaced vanity was what made me realise that continuing to deny that my head isn't very good at making hair would just lead me into that same kind of spiral. That man never looked like someone who had hair. He looked like someone wearing a wig. Which always felt to me like a less dignified position than someone who doesn't have any hair. And so I decided to embrace that, I think—just shave it off and have more dignity.

But that discomfort with how I looked remained and, if anything, it became even harder to ignore internally. Is it a Weight Watchers trope where they talk about, *Oh, you're a thin person inside a fat person's body trying to get out?* Unhelpful crap. [But] I feel like a man with luscious floppy hair in a bald man's body. And I suppose it's the finality of my baldness that I find most upsetting. Like, there's no way in my future I will be able to change it. It's something I'm unhappy about but it's impossible to change. I suppose I'd feel more confident and just more comfortable generally if I had the same kind of hair in my waking hours as I do in a lot of my dreams. Those feelings haven't gone away.

And I can understand a lot better now how someone starts wearing a wig in their twenties and ends up wearing it for four decades, despite every single person they meet knowing that they're bald. So if anything I have a lot more sympathy for my aunt's husband than I ever expected I would. I still very much wish I had hair. And every day it's something that I have to confront—that I'm older than I'd like to be, that I'm bald and wouldn't like to be—and that is something that I feel like I'm publicly denying by shaving my head. If anything it compounds it. I think the uncle I mentioned, he probably feels like he doesn't look bald. It's the difference between internal and external. I'm not trying to pretend I have hair, but in doing that I'm implying I'm comfortable when I'm not. Whereas he's doing the opposite. So he feels comfortable even though he looks uncomfortable to others.

How's your hairline?

107.

My father used to say, *Even though you have a problem, you don't show it to people. You keep your head up and smile.*

Nobody knows. There's a lot of people, they wouldn't know everything I'm telling you, my life. They don't know. They think everything is perfect for me. Because they think of my dad, how he was before, without them knowing that when he left we lost everything. They think that, even though he's not here, my life is just perfect. I like that. I don't want people feeling pity for me.

Not because he's my father, but he was an incredible person. I used to call him my hero. When he want to be a funny man he was very funny. When it's time to be a strict father, he would be strict father. He was a very gentle man. When your daughter, your child do something, maybe you can slap them, just to make them stop. My father didn't. My father would just not talk to you. Then I know he's not happy! He might not even talk to me for a week [laughs]. Especially when I start growing up and becoming a teenager, yeah, this kind of punishment was very strict. He wouldn't talk to me, he wouldn't give me my pocket money [laughs]. Until you learn your lesson that, yes, you done something very, very wrong. If I write something, even though French is my first language, I write a letter to my father, the letter would come back with a lot of correction [laughs]. To tell you how it was! Even though I miss an accent—you know in French sometimes you have to put some apostrophe? If

I miss one he will send me my letter back. That it's rubbish [laughs]. But in reality he was a very good man. He was a very gentle man. In his family, he look after everybody. Funny enough, when he died, there was nobody to look after him. Can you believe that? That's what's always making me sad. Because there was nobody there. None of his family member, none of his close people that did love him truly.

I don't think it was a natural death or a sickness. Because he never been sick. We believe he was poisoned by the other side, the government side. My dad, first of all, naturally was a journalist, before becoming a politician—so when he talk he didn't fear, he just criticise them. Because you know in Africa it's not like here. You can wake up in the morning and criticise Boris Johnson, nobody will arrest you. But in Africa, in _____, you criticise a president or anybody that have power, the next day they can kill you. He was still making noise. Criticising them, writing article. So we believe that he was killed. He went to our embassy to ask for a visa—he wanted to go to France. That day that he went to the embassy and then he went back to his hotel, that's when he had a problem. So, for me, he was killed. I don't have proof. Which I've been telling them. I was not there. But it is true that my dad was killed.

It's a very sad story because I never got a chance to say goodbye. Imagine your father died in a different country, where he doesn't have family there, not his wife or children, no member of the family. It's very traumatic. I don't like talking about it. I did my best to try and ask if I could go and say goodbye, but I couldn't. Cos if I did then I just have to remain in _____. And I can't remain in _____, because I have nothing, I have nobody, I'm not safe. So I never got the chance to say goodbye. I was relying on somebody there to find out if he's presentable, how is the coffin to look like, the day they were taking his body home, who's going to be there. So that's the story. I will be very happy, one day, even just to see the place they buried him. But I been in a kind of cage.

108.

I'm a pretty anxious person. I get afraid of different things at different times. Like if I'm hungover, I get really worried that there'll be some sort of violent act against me. If I'm hungover and I'm sat on the tube, I'll think that the person across from me is just gonna grab me by the throat or something. It'll go away, it doesn't consume me or anything, it's just for a second and then it'll go. But I find, even when nothing goes wrong in the end, it still leaves me a little bit shook up, if that makes sense? I think the thing with those kind of exaggerated fears is that once you start feeling them, you spend a lot of time consumed by them and thinking about them. And then it becomes harder for you to regard them as unimportant. Like, it's weird to spend a week consumed by something and worried by something and then at the end of the week it's just gone and it never mattered— you didn't need to plan for that thing happening cos it wasn't real in the first place.

With anxiety I think you are able to sort of step out of yourself and recognise it as anxiety, and for me that helps. I went away earlier this year—when you still could—and I knew that because of a week of drinking quite a lot, I knew when I came back I would be anxious about the weekend just gone. I just knew it. So as soon as it came I was able to go, *Well, here it is, looks like a hangover to get through*, which sort of helped. Cos even though you're aware of it, it's still not a fun place to be. You can't sit back and laugh at it, but if you know that's the process then at least you're familiar with what's gonna happen.

When I had really bad OCD I went to a therapist for a while, just because I wasn't functioning. He gave me this exercise that was to write down all the things that made me anxious, all the things that I was afraid of, and he had me sort of rank them from the worst one to the least worst one. And he told me to sit in my room and look at them for fifteen minutes. I literally put an egg timer on and then I just stared at this list and I thought about all of those things in the most graphic detail I possibly could for a really horrible fifteen minutes and then, when the timer went, I put the piece of paper in a drawer and it was just gone for the day. It didn't cure me or anything but it was a way of going, *If you're gonna have these thoughts, if you're gonna be afraid of certain things, be afraid of them, fine, but be in control of it as well.* And it did sort of help to go, *Okay, you've had your fifteen minutes,* you know? *Fuck off now* [laughs].

[One of the things with] anxiety and OCD was accepting that it's gonna be there a bit. If you can get to 10 per cent rather than 90 per cent, it's probably fine. That's probably a more realistic expectation than it being totally gone. I really suffered from OCD when I was twenty, and it's so weird now to look back on diary entries of things I was worried about, and I can't even make the connection. I came across [one] where I'd spoken about putting hand sanitiser over coins and notes before giving them to someone at Tesco, and when I read it I thought, *I can't even remember why I was doing that, what the actual thought was,* and it's so good to get to the point where, yeah, you still worry about missing the train or whatever, but I'm not washing money before I hand it over to someone in Tesco. And I can't even remember why I was doing that. So great, that's a victory, in a big sense.

109.

I think this week feels like we are slowly crawling towards a light at the end of the tunnel. That's probably a universal feeling that is being experienced by a lot of people. It feels like we've been in stasis for some time. I feel like I've been in stasis for the past [laughs] ten months, but maybe I've been in stasis for more than that—over a year, a year and a half. It feels like we are coming towards a resolution. We are seeing some sort of real hope on the horizon. Whether that's temporary, we don't know. But it's definitely something, it's more than we've seen this year.

In some ways this resolution has made me feel like I'm biding time even more because I'm waiting to reach that light. And that is frustrating. I think for everyone, the past few months—especially the last lockdown here in the UK—has got even more frustrating cos we've been through this before. We know the pattern, we know the rubric of what this is going to do to our daily lives, and our interactions and our emotions and our physicality—the way we physically can relate to people in the world. We've been through this. In staying in the day-to-day, or the hour-to-hour, or the minute-to-minute, I am having to numb myself because I can't plan my future. And in some ways that removes for me the idea of hope or [laughs] the ability to project, the ability to fantasise, the ability to *want*, because it's all just so fucking unknown.

Although this year has completely torn apart the fabric of my life in pretty much every single possible way it could have done, I am still here. I'm still around. I still have a network, I still have some family, great friends, a home, and the ability to survive. So that's very humbling and I feel very grateful for that. And I feel very grateful for my body—that it's kept me alive throughout this and it's kept me alive throughout the thirty-five years that I've been here. That's definitely a beautiful thing to think about.

I definitely feel like throughout maybe the last four to five years, that we've been living through an incredible amount of change—the kind of change that I think my parents would have seen in the sixties, seventies. Socially, in terms of what it means to be a woman, in terms of what it means to be on a spectrum of sexuality, in terms of what it means to be a Black person living in a predominantly white Western society. The kind of communication that people are having is fascinating. It's like nothing I've ever had in my life. I feel like communication is more transparent than it's ever been. And that is really fucking exciting. That feels really powerful. I feel empowered by the dialogue. That's fascinating and that's exciting and that's encouraging. It encourages me to think that kids that I see growing up now are gonna have a much more nuanced idea of who they are and what they can be. And they're gonna feel less boundaries on themselves. That's an amazing feeling—that I am living through a time that is opening up these possibilities.

I do still feel lucky. I feel lucky. I think that in the thirty-five years that I've inhabited this planet, this has been, without a doubt, the hardest year I've ever experienced. I thought previously that might be 2015 or 2019. But this is, obviously, for most people alive right now, the hardest year we've ever experienced. Perhaps universally, collectively, as a group. But that also brings with it a unification, to some degree. And feeling that is incredibly comforting. I know that I'm going to be very different. I feel very different from who I was in December 2019. I feel like this year has completely changed my outlook on what I want to do. Who I want to be.

110

We used to say that when we look at somebody, to imagine it's a chest of drawers. What's on the top—you know, the vases or whatever you have on the top—is what you see immediately. That's how you present to the world and how people see you. Then there's what's in the top drawer, and then as you get to know someone a bit more, you might learn what's in the second drawer. Then of course we used to all have a laugh about what's under the rug and the floorboards at the bottom [laughs], that nobody knows about. You can take the analogy as far as you like, can't you? There's the stuff that nobody sees. I like that analogy. It's a good exercise to think about how we see people.

I've recently changed what I look like. I've always dyed my hair brown with streaks of different colour so it looks really natural, so most people have thought that this is my natural colour. Been colouring it since I was twenty-five, I suppose—went grey very early and when I was working, I used to get one every three weeks, cos I had quite a big job and had to look nice and smart, suited and all that. When Covid started—cos I was seventy in January—because I couldn't go to the hairdresser I thought, *Do I colour it myself?* No, I didn't wanna do that, haven't done that for years. So a lot of people who are seeing me now haven't seen me since March or February, I think they're thinking, *Oh my goodness, you look so old now.* Which is interesting, but actually I don't care. I've had it cut short to try and get the dye out, there's just a little bit of it left, which is toned down. Now, when I look in the mirror, I see my sister, who's older than me, I see my cousin, I see my mum, and I've never seen those before. I've embraced the natural colour, which I didn't know was as white as this. I thought it might be grey, but it's white. And I'm not gonna go back now, this is it. I'm gonna save such a lot of money, such a lot of time, such a lot of effort. I used to constantly be straightening it, using all products, now I just wash it, rub it, it waves, it curls.

It sounds rather arrogant but I had a big job managing a lot of people, and massive turnover, and when people saw me who didn't know me, they immediately assumed that I didn't. If I said I worked in the care sector, which is what I did, they would say, *What, were you a care assistant?* I like cars, and so I'd go and look for a car, and they would assume I couldn't afford one. Makes me quite emotional when I think about it. Probably also because of the way I speak as well, because it's a bit Estuary, a bit Essex, a bit London, you know, which I'm fine about, absolutely fine about. Especially as you get older as a woman, they assume. I actually had to go to hospital for an emergency a few weeks ago and I'd gone with no make-up on and white hair and my old-lady look—looked scruffy, cos I'd had to go quickly so I'd just chucked a trackie on. And this consultant, she's talking to me like this, infantilisation here, I could've slapped her. You know, *Sorry, do you work?* She guessed I didn't, so I said, *Yeah, I do a bit of consultancy but I'm retired from full-time work.* I just gave it to her both barrels, which I don't often do. I won't say it to you, but the title and whatever, how many million pounds turnover I ran and whatever. And her and this young doctor both went, *Wow*, and they immediately treated me differently.

111.

I guess I was about ten at the time. I went on holiday one summer with my mum and brother, and also my uncle and aunt and my two cousins. We all stayed in a big house in France together. My uncle hired a car, which we could use to drive to the local shops.

One day, me and my mum drove out to the shops together. The place we were staying was at the bottom of a hill. There was a road down to the gate of the house. I don't quite remember how this came about, but when we got to the top of the hill I asked my mum if I could sit in the driver's seat and drive the car down to the bottom of the hill. Drive it as in with the engine off, so that basically it was just freewheeling. For some reason my mum agreed and I got into the driver's seat and because my legs were too short to reach the brakes, my mum just told me to use the handbrake as we got near the bottom of the hill.

I sat in the driver's seat and we went down this hill and as we got nearer the front, I pulled on the handbrake. And nothing happened. The car just kept rolling. It was going pretty slowly, but there was a car parked in the road and, basically, our car banged into the back of this other car, bumper to bumper, and stopped. And I remember, there was a moment of shock and then my mum saying, *Get into the back! Get into the back!* And I undid the seat belt and jumped into the back seat and my mum moved across into the driver's seat. And about that moment, my uncle and aunt came running out of the house, cos they heard this noise, to try and see what was going on. And they said, *What happened?!* My mum said, *Oh, I, er, I crashed.* She made out that she was a bit confused and they said to me, *Are you okay? Were you thrown forward? Because I thought I saw you having to climb back into the back?* And my mum said, *Oh, no, no, he's fine,* and I said, *No, I'm fine.* And basically, this secret was made between me and my mum—that I was the one that had crashed this car and that she'd covered for me.

Sometimes, later on, when I used to argue with my mum, in the middle of the argument she would say to me, *And I covered for you that time when you crashed your uncle's car!* I used to be torn apart when she said that. I was in floods of tears. I said, *Why did you remind me? I'm trying to forget!* I used to hate visiting my uncle and aunt after that, because I always felt that somehow they were suspicious of me, that they probably knew what had happened but didn't say anything. And I think it really coloured my relationship to them growing up.

That was the secret that I carried with me and I have a coda to it. When I was in my early twenties, I told a friend this story and she said to me, *Oh, how horrible of your mum to make you cover up for her like that!* And I was really shocked. I spent my whole childhood thinking that my mum had covered up for me for this terrible thing I'd done. And suddenly I realised that actually my mum hadn't been covering up for me—I'd been covering up for my mum. That it was she who didn't want it to get out that she'd allowed me to drive the rent-a-car. It was a shocking moment for me, and this secret, that I'd lived with for all of these years, was suddenly turned around.

112.

It looked like a little, deflated or soggy, saggy water balloon.
The texture of a very thin outer layer, almost like a waterbed.
And it looked sort of opaque, but not really. It was difficult
to see what it looked like, actually, because it was covered in
a lot of blood. And it was only a flashing moment in which I
did get to see it.

The second response is what it looked like in my dream of
it thereafter, which will probably give more of a clue of what
it might be. It looked like a tiny, alien form. It looked slightly
reptilian, or fishlike. And it looked like it was going to be an
invasive creature of which I would be a host. Not necessarily
through choice. It looked [hesitates] very personable. This
is in my dream. It looked like a complete entity. It looked
like a globule or a sphere, or a planet—a biological planet, of
possibility, creation, hibernation. A world unto its own. And
it was very fleeting [laughs] when I saw it.

In April of this year, I had a miscarriage at twelve weeks
and so what passed through me was the, I think it's some
sort of sac, I can't remember what it's called, but with the
amniotic fluid and everything else like that. So that's where
the image of a water balloon—very delicate—comes from.
And it obviously passed through me very quickly and so
that's what I saw—this bloody but delicate globe. But then I
dreamt of that experience three or four times and it looked
very different—and more obviously developed—in my
subconscious mind, what that little globe, sac, encompassed.

The imagery was consistent, which I think is interesting. This globe—I keep doing this with my hands, demonstrating it. But also in cosmic terms, a star or a potential planet. Everything that can be held within this void, this potential for creation.

I think in a way I disassociated myself from it. What did it look like? It was just this water balloon of a parallel universe, of a secondary option. It kind of represents a lot of chaos, as well. We were going through a lot of chaos and confusion globally and it just went one way. You know when you drop the marble, or a coin, into a pin machine and each option branches out and then you end up with multiple options at the bottom? But it all starts from the same point? It's a bit like one of those. Or like the lottery, when you have all the different balls, numbered ping pong balls or whatever, jumbling around.

One thing I found really interesting in China, when I toured China for six weeks, was their relationship with luck, chance, serendipity. They will bet on anything. They really like this idea of some sort of external chaos just happening. And then you take your chances which way it goes. They'll even bet on picking two raindrops on a window and seeing which one will get down the furthest or which one will cross over to the far left of the pane, or the far right, or whatever. It has to be very instinctive and immediate. You set up those parameters really quickly but then you sit and observe the chaos playing out. Or the luck playing out. Or the chance playing out. And your relationship with that is very interesting. It doesn't really matter which way chance goes—it is your relationship with chaotic events that defines the experience. There's a song that revolved around my head a lot. It's 'Que Sera Sera'. [Sings the refrain then pauses for a moment.] There's something quite nice about that release or letting go. I think I averted a lot more [laughs] trauma and psychological pain by readjusting my relationship with chaos.

113

My grandfather on my mother's side was a very religious man. When I first went to university, I suppose at eighteen, he wrote me a letter talking to me about how he'd gone to Bible college at the age of eighteen, in the Rhondda Valley, but had had to come back because his father was a terrible businessman. Which unfortunately ran in the family, because then my grandfather had to take over the family business, which was growing tomatoes in _____ , and he wasn't any good at it, either. So at about the age of fifty, I suppose, probably the age I am now, the business collapsed, as I understand it, but he fulfilled his life's ambition and became a reverend in the church, which he then did before he retired.

By the time I was twenty he was really quite unwell. He'd had a number of strokes, and he used to come and visit us, often for Christmas, and in fact that's the last time I saw him. He was obviously quite horrified about exactly what Christmas entailed for me at that point, which was, to put it bluntly, irreligious—very much about going out, going to the pub, probably drinking excessively—and this had clearly worried him. I went to say goodbye to him in the bedroom—I was going off to school that day, he must've been going home. And unfortunately, the last thing he said to me was, *You know, _____ , you will understand one day that Christmas is a Christian festival.* And I don't think I knew what to say, so I think unfortunately that's the last conversation we ever had. I guess also unfortunately, from his point of view, as it turns out I couldn't be further away from that now. So it didn't actually happen at all.

But it revealed a side to my grandfather which I hadn't ever seen before, really. He wasn't as much fun as my grandmother, he wasn't as engaged with us, but he always seemed very nice. And, in fact, niceness was my grandfather's way of managing life. He was a reverend, he was just nice to everybody. To the point, actually, of blandness, I have to say. So when he suddenly came out with something so heartfelt and so strong, I remember feeling really shocked. Which makes it sad in that unfortunately we didn't manage to carry on and have other conversations. Although I don't think he would've been able to have a conversation about how I didn't really believe. I mean, at that point I'm not sure I knew what I believed, but certainly as things have gone on, I'm completely sure that I'm not a Christian. After he died, I went to the funeral, and I remember seeing some of his diaries that my mum and my uncle had dug out, and they were astonishing. He would literally write, apart from a report on the weather every day, he would literally write, several times a week, *I'm so happy that Jesus is alive!* That's the sort of thing he would write in his diary.

When you're young, having a grandparent is just another fun adult who dotes on you. And then, when you're an adolescent you're not very interested in them. I'm sad I didn't get a chance to be an adult who might've been interested. And I never got to talk to him about that. It seems astonishing how religious he was. It was the centre of his whole being. And I guess it eventually exploded out of him. And, against his character, he said what he finally thought. And it's sad that it's the last thing that was ever there. I don't know what that means. Perhaps it means that, even at the last, people can still surprise you [laughs]. Cos it certainly surprised me.

114.

I loved lockdown so much. I wanna go back. I loved it. I
enjoyed the simplicity. I got to know myself better, and got to
rely on myself a little better, so I loved the lockdown thing. It
was hard, but it felt necessary. You can't walk around with a
giant splinter in your foot the rest of your life, you've got to
eventually take it out. You can't be walking in pain.

My husband—shall I say ex-husband?—has suffered from
mental health issues for the majority of his life. I knew this
when we met. At that point he was on medication and getting
help from therapy and lots of support. How am I gonna put
this? I think the anxiety was incredibly hard on him during
lockdown. There was no medication apart from therapy, he
just went up and down. Many things happened, many toxic
things happened, and it kind of escalated to a critical point
where I recognised that this was an abusive situation and
was having an impact on the three boys. My husband, my
ex-husband, has two children from a previous marriage, and
they were witnessing this abusive dynamic. My son, who's
eight—and this is probably the biggest change in my life—
his fists were clenched, and he's like, *Mummy, just do what
he says. Do what he says.* And I just kinda felt, *This is it. This
is the end.*

Everything that had ever happened in a period of ten years
had to be displayed to loads of different organisations and
support networks. This was right when Black Lives Matter
happened. The police had to come cos they had to do a

welfare assessment, and I was in the back of a police car when George Floyd had died the week before. And it was kinda like, *Please don't kill me*, like I'm joking, but I'm not joking, cos I'm a Black woman in the back of your car. And the police officer was really sensitive: *Don't worry, I get it, this is scary for you, this is all very scary.* Now we're in the process of sorting out our living situation, that's the key bit, which has been agreed between us, but we have to get all the financial bits done. Divorce paperwork is in. We get along again, now, but again it's chemical, so he can switch. There's a strong possibility that before he ends up moving out, there will be another situation. Which is unfortunate.

This brings up a lot of firsts for me. This is the first time organising the purchase of a house on my own. I never thought I'd be a single mother, never thought I would be considering myself as a survivor of domestic abuse and violence. I would never have thought these things were ever gonna occur in my life. But then I'm really grateful to it because there's so much I can offer—and so many people share this. It's a period of history where we're being much more honest about our personal experience with mental health issues. There was a time when this would not have been considered a crime. Men could practically kill their wives and it would not be considered a crime. I think there's probably a stage of grief that's happening. Obviously it's not linear. There's been a lot of grief, anger, resentment, loneliness, and then comes the solution, right? The solution is, *How do I lift myself out of this, and what do I need to be able to do that?* And I feel very, very supported, so the reason why I probably look like I'm handling it well is because I have a huge, huge, huge amount of support. Isolation is the biggest factor of abusive relationships. I have been separated from everyone.

115

They come two o'clock night. They put handcuff on me. They took me to the airport, they took me on the plane. I don't wanna go. I was crying. I say that I don't want to go, I fear for my life. They beat me up! They handcuff me behind my back, they was punching me. They put my head down like this, three of them. I was feeling pain. It's like I'm gonna die. They beat me badly until the passenger start to come. One woman come and said, *I can hear somebody screaming.* I was sweating. She took a cloth to wipe my sweat and asked them why are they treating me like this? They said I'm asylum seeker, my case has been refused. She says, *Because asylum seeker you treat him this way?!* The woman ask them for their ID, but they refuse to give it. And then the woman gave me her phone number. She said they need to let me call her. When we get to Belgium, they took me, they put the handcuff on me and then they took me to a cell. Then they took the card that the woman gave to me. They took it off me. They never gave me back. And then they took me to _____ _____. I could not even stand and talk. Blood on my jacket.

I don't know what was going on, the officers they come to me like, *We're coming back here.* I was tired. I was all by myself. And then they brought me back here. They brought me back. They said to me I have to thumbprint a document. I said, *No! I fear to go back.* They beat me there. In the nighttime they took me to detention. Then after some weeks, they release me, then I went back to _____ , where I used to live. They told me to sign. I was signing, signing, then they arrest me again. When they arrest me again, that's the time they detain me for three years.

After two months they said to me I'm not complying. And then they took me from detention and they charge me. They said because I'm not complying to go back, it's a crime. It's an offence. And then they took me to prison! We went to court and they found me guilty, then the judge give me eighteen months prison sentence. I did not steal anything in the street, I did not fight anybody or do any bad things to anybody. I'm just asylum seeker. People keep coming to me, ask me what I'm in for. When I told them it's this thing, they looking me like, *No, you must have done something.* Except I haven't. It's very, very scary. Very intimidating. You see a lot of things. You see people fighting there. You see they can throw hot water on you in prison. Boiling water! They put sugar there and throw it on you. It's not a good place.

Detention is another prison as well. It's the same. They moved me from there, took me to prison, which is the hardest, so I'm thinking, *Okay, maybe when I finish here, they will release me.* But they did not. They take me again and bring me back to detention. I break down. And up till now I'm in medication. Yeah, I'm in medication. I just wanna live a normal and a peaceful life. I'm a human being, you know? I don't go starting trouble to anybody. I believe I have the right to live a peaceful, normal life. Like anyone. It's disturbing my head thinking about my life. I don't have

my paper to live my peaceful life, a normal life. I don't
deserve it. I don't deserve it.

116.

It's how you control. It's how the government works. Everything we see before us in the world that's wrong, it's because of people doing that. That's how the world spins, and that's pretty much the crux of what's wrong with everything. Cos if that wasn't a culture of how things are done then you wouldn't have as many folks just going along not making up their own minds and regurgitating shit. Belief is the ultimate, one of the most powerful, effective ways of doing exactly that—manipulating others. You make them believe shit.

I avoid the word *belief* when it comes to my own self. As in, I have an understanding of things, I have an awareness of things, I have an idea of things. Belief is never, never in the equation. Belief was when you're a kid, and there's still some things you don't have enough data, evidence, answers, conversations about, that you just have to believe it. I feel that at this point, it's more important than ever that folks don't believe. If I had to do that, the context would be I'm villainous. That would be the only reason I would want someone to believe something without me proving it, or showing and proving, or without there being any evidence, any objective validity to it, you know?

When you say *we*, that *we* doesn't exist. Pakistan, which is my nation of birth, technically speaking, is not a country. There's no *we*. There's a set of different tribes, some feudal, some not, some city folks. There's four or five distinct areas with their own identities, and some of them don't even rep the nation. There's no *we* there. Ideologically speaking, as we move forward, I feel that society is gonna schism into islands, ideological islands. You've already got the inequality between the city-states—you know, the capital cities, the city-states—and rural areas or poor areas of Black and Brown countries that have been colonised and are still poor. But then within that, you'll have so many opposing views that are incompatible to live alongside. Look at the anti-vaxxers, versus *We will take every vaccine you give us*, right? That's mutually exclusive—you cannot co-exist, right? Practically, it's not possible. My point is that there is such a lack of a *we* that—not on a eugenics level, but on an ideological level—folks may as well be alien to each other. This is why—as society fractures and becomes more schismed and your own best friends and family have views that you thought they wouldn't be capable of holding—the need for an antithesis to belief and faith is even more important. Cos not enough folks are critical. I'm saying that word as a skill, not as an emotion or an intent, as a skill: problem-solving and learning to adapt and learning to disseminate from information and use it in a meaningful way.

It's absolutely essential that the folks in the world who are currently not the ones with power, who aren't the elite, those who are victims of racism, oppression, classism, gender, whatever—and particularly those people who don't have access to institutionalised learning—it's imperative that they become personal scientists. Because the choices that will be made for society on their behalf going forward will be even more graver than anything that is done on our behalf at the moment. And the only way to navigate that successfully is through being a self-scientist. And not the cold, institutional version of it. The version that celebrates the joy of learning, exploring, and solving problems. Let's go explain the unexplained which is magical, unbelievable, or miraculous, or paranormal, or supernatural—cos that's just tomorrow's science and understanding.

117

I've got a twin. We're like best friends, but also the most different two people you've ever met, like chalk and cheese. That was what my dad always said. So I would say it wouldn't be losing her, it would be the not having her. It's a strange thought. It's not so much the experience of loss—I would be scared about my life rather than the event. And very linked to that is probably losing your sense of self. Or not knowing who I am. Because I think I would probably just disassociate. I know who I am and everything. And I know who she is. But I rely very heavily on her perception of me. I get a lot out of that. It seems selfish because it is about having her in my life, that's obviously a huge thing. But at the end of the day, it's really hard to try and separate that from how it makes you feel. And how it contributes to your identity, or your being real. Because it's not just beauty that's in the eye of the beholder. It's everything.

We didn't walk until we were quite old. Mum had walked when she was really young. And spoke. But we just sat in the buggy going, *Urrrrr*. And that's kind of what we do now. It's different with twins—you don't need as much stimuli because you are each other's stimuli. I think that's the best way to describe it, as little young things, little animals. Yes, there's the world around you but there's also somebody stood or sat right in front of you that kind of looks like you. And as much as your child brain can process that, I think that's really interesting. Because if you have an older sibling, you're a part of their world. You see them walking around and exploring and you're jealous and you want to be part of that. Whereas if you're the same age, you don't really have that.

I'm used to being completely understood by [my sister]. I think the bar's set high for relationships as well. That's another fear, especially romantically, I think—not finding something that is as important. And obviously, that's a really stupid standard to set because it's never going to happen. Being able to connect with someone like that? I would have to spend my entire life with someone to get that. I know if I'm acting up or I've changed or I start getting loads of piercings or whatever, she'll just be like, *What you think you're doing?* She's so sharp and clever and mean. She'll be like, *The fuck are you doing? What's going on?* And I'll be like, *Argh, I should not do that.*

I think people expect this closeness to be represented in things like talking all the time—y'know, talking about your feelings. We never, neither of us, has ever liked the idea of being constantly available, which is what I kind of hate about having the phone on all the time and being involved in a realm, virtually, that you can't really get out of. We only started hugging when we left home. People assume that because we spend so much time together, it's a really luvvy-duvvy kind of close sibling relationship. And it's not. It's not like that. I think I miss her the most when I'm either in a bit of a slump or not doing lots of interesting things. Or if I know she is. It generally just equates to FOMO, really—twin FOMO.

118

I'm someone who finds it very hard to climax penetratively, and I worry about that a lot when I have sex with people, because there will be that moment when they'll realise that it's just not happening. And then I'll be like, *Okay, I'm going to have to fake it or something cos I'm tired now* [laughs]. I mean, penetrative sex is always pleasurable for me in the first two minutes [laughs] and then after that it just gets a bit tiring—because there's just not much else going on for me. There has been some partners who have been more considerate and will spend more time thinking about other things, other ways to approach my body. And those are always the more favourable experiences. However, because I have quite a lot of different partners, I don't always have control over if that's how that person's going to be. You never know how someone's going to be in bed until you have sex with them. And I think it's still quite difficult for me to ask for what I want, because I think I still have these ingrained attitudes of sex being penetrative and that's all that sex is. Like, it all comes down to this moment. So I do still struggle with that.

I mean, there's always that desire for me to have sex. Always. And it's always such a disappointment, you know— it's bigger in your head than it is in life. Saying that, it does bring me closer to people. I do like that closeness with people, but I no longer feel that need of being in a relationship with someone after having sex with them. I don't rate that kind of attachment. There was only one year of my life where I had a stable sex partner. That was the first time I had sex. I never had sex before then. And so I sort of discovered this inability, if you would, that I have, of climaxing penetratively. I was like, *Well, what's wrong? I really love this person. We have such great attraction, such great chemistry.* And I think we were too young for (a) him to be openly communicative about his frustrations with it and (b) me to be open about—*I don't know what's going on with my body!* You know, when you're first having sex, you've no idea what's going on. You don't really know your arsehole from your earhole [laughs]. But even after a year and a half of it, I was still just so stuck in that: *I just don't know what's wrong with me,* you know? *How can I change this?* And I think it grew more and more frustrating for him. I think that has marked me for the rest of my life [laughs], because that relationship ended so badly, [and] in a way I think I blamed it on this inability that I had. I couldn't give my partner what he wanted, which was to make me climax. I don't know, it's always sort of tarnished it for me a bit. Which brings me back to this thing of vulnerability, why I feel so vulnerable within sex. It's because I can never climax. It just makes me think always about this long relationship I had, that I loved, that fell apart. And even though there was probably a million reasons why it fell apart, a big part of it to me felt like it was because we just weren't managing that well. At least I wasn't.

119

I got caught speeding on a motorbike and I was gonna go to court for reasons of this very naughty speed. My barrister said, *What do you do?* And I said, *Oh, I drive white vans.*

You drive white vans?! Whatever you do, you need to quit now cos they're gonna take your licence away. They hate white van man and they hate people on motorbikes. And you are both. You are stuffed. You tear past them in their Mercedes and put two fingers up. You need to go and find a job that will look good in court.

I had a friend who worked with children with epilepsy. Then he started working in regular children's homes (there's nothing regular about them but I'll call them regular). And he said, *Come and have a go at this!* I told my barrister and he goes, *Right, you've got to do it. You need to do a week and then you can call it your profession.*

He made me write this horrible, cringey letter about what a wonderful human I am. And he says, *Do what I tell you. Go in there and say you're sorry. Do not say you're sorry for speeding. The speed you were doing, you were loving it and the magistrates will know you love it because you were going that fast. But,* he said, *no one else will have said sorry today.* And I was like, *Are you joking?!* He said, *You tell me.*

So I go in there, I say I was sorry, hand them the letter. One of the magistrates threw my letter on the floor and one of them gave me the evils throughout. But the chairman and one of the others actually read it. And they go, *This is a serious business, we're going to deliberate.* I was like, *He hates me. He proper hates me! This is the worst day ever.* Anyway, they go in and they come back and they go, *You've been a very naughty boy. Here's six points and a fifty-pound fine.* And court costs, that was like twenty quid or something. They say, *Don't do it again and off you go.* And that was it.

That was how I became a childcare officer. I go and do the job for a week and I loved it. I really, really like the young people I look after. And they are very violent, they are very aggressive, they do silly things, but when you know them, you know it's about hurting themselves and not feeling worthy of anything else. And when you hear what's happened to them, you're like, *Of course you do this. Of course you would. Why wouldn't you? That's all you've known.*

I've had some real moments of beauty. I was once in the car and we were listening to stuff on my phone and there's some church worship music. And this girl I was with, she's like, *Oh, what is this?! You loser!* It was a little bit stronger than that, obviously. She starts listening to it. And then she starts singing along to it.

When we get to the end of the journey she goes, *What the heck was that?*

I was like, *I don't know what you mean.*

And she goes, *Whilst I was singing that, I felt clean and beautiful.*

275

She looked me right in the eyes. I'm already choking up.
And she goes, *You know, I've never felt clean and beautiful in my life before.*

120.

[If] we live in a deterministic universe and everything is governed by a system of cause and effect, [that] negates the idea of you having free will. Every action that happens is determined by a previous cause, and every action that you take is determined by that action that happened before. I have no idea, nor the intellect, to wonder how you would actually make it provable. What level of maths and complexity of maths you would need to figure out that the universe is deterministic is beyond me. To quote that famous cliché around quantum mechanics—if you think you understand quantum mechanics, you don't understand quantum mechanics. And that's the reality, is that we don't understand how something works at a quantum level, what makes it workable in a world where we have general relativity, special relativity, things that follow standard physics.

I think the world and the universe is so utterly random at times, and the minute that you think that you've got a grasp on it, it just falls away, almost ridicules you. So from a personal perspective, the idea of determinism makes sense to me and my subjective experience of my life. I think determinism is more philosophical rather than scientific, but the idea that it might be unprovable is what appeals to me about it. There's a kind of misunderstanding that science means that something is provable, where my understanding is that it's about falsifiability. You know, the idea that the fundamental nature of it is that we don't actually know, but let's go on a journey, and let's see what we can find out. Also, determinism doesn't mean pre-determinism—don't say that it's pre-determined, that something created it that pre-determined every outcome.

I think there are certain things that happened that I don't feel like I could've changed. I just don't. Those things, they were there, they happened, and they led to that, which led to that set of events, which then led to that next set of events, which got me here. Obviously there's an amount of luck in there, but it is completely subjective in that if I think of certain events that happened to me, particularly in my teenage years, my early twenties, it's almost like they had to happen. It's just an inevitability. It's almost like I had to go to the places I had to go to to learn the things that I did. It's difficult to put into words—they were the feelings I had to experience for me to make the next step. The minute I took certain actions, the consequence was inevitable, it was almost determined. That's the other thing I like about determinism and also the illusion of free will—the minute I think I'm in the driving seat, I realise that I'm not in the driving seat [laughs]. You know, there's something else that's going along here, that's taking it somewhere, and I'm just a passenger. I'm definitely a passenger that's just on this journey. You're not in the driving seat. Your life is within that determinism, and within that sense of nothing really being there. Apart from, you know, love, empathy, compassion, the beautiful calmness of being a human being, I suppose. You know, gratitude, fun, those kind of things. Bill Hicks said it, he put it beautifully: *Enjoy the ride.*

121.

I must admit I'm not a book person. Newspapers, I sit and read newspapers, but I've never been a book person. I will sit and look at a map book, which people think's quite sad, but that's just the nature of the job, I suppose.

I like to look at my maps, especially if I'm going to London. I know my way round London very well, I would say, as a coach driver, but I always like to know where I'm going. So if I was going London at the weekend, when I'm down here at the airport for an hour waiting for a plane to come in, I'll get my map out. I'll look, do my homework, where I'm gonna drop off, where I'm gonna park and all stuff like that. As a coach driver you're meant to be a professional driver so I like to do it—be professional, be prepared. I've been in the industry for thirty-seven years and I'm still going new places. Last week I had a school party to Crocodile World and I've never been there in my life!

I take a wide variety of people. One day I could be taking a load of older people down to near Yarmouth for the bowling for a five-day and then the following week I could be taking a load of eighteen-year-olds to an airport or people on a hen do or stag do. I like to think I adapt to the group, if you know what I mean. Cos at the end of the day most people are going for leisure. I like to try and make their trip as enjoyable as possible. They've chosen to go there as a hobby or a pastime or for fun. Whether it be a church group or a load of lads going on a stag do for a day, they're all going to have a day out and it's their leisure time, and I try to make it as enjoyable as I can.

It's quite interesting when you're driving a coach, cos you can sit in the driver's seat and you can keep your ears open and you can hear people behind talking. And you're sort of earwigging what they're talking about. It's interesting. People are interesting, aren't they? That's why I like my job. What is one person's good day out is not another person's good day out. But I take so many different people I just adapt and go and have a look round and see what they're doing. I've had times in my life where I've been really stressed out about things, I've had times where you're really happy and you don't sort of care. Sitting in the coach, drifting, thinking things. Sometimes you sit there and think, *God, my life's good*, and other days you'll think, *It's a mess*. You're stressed about the bad things in your life, you don't stress about the good things, so I suppose the point is if you're sitting there reflecting or thinking about your life and what you're gonna do, think about the good things. The good things that are coming up. You know. Enjoy the good things and don't worry about the bad things.

Full of crocodiles, really! Fifteen species of crocodile, yeah.

122.

I gotta get up for the dog. And the kids. I've gotta take my youngest to school. And I work so, you know, I've got reasons to get up in the morning. Would I choose to do all of those if I was financially secure? I probably wouldn't get up for work [laughs]. And anyone who says they would is lying. Because, you know, we're not put on this planet to get up at nine o'clock and work till five every day, are we? I think we're probably designed to sit about in a field eating mushrooms and fucking each other's brains out all day. I mean, at a fundamental level that's probably what we would do if we didn't have the construct of capitalism, isn't it?

What we need and what we get are two completely different things. I don't need a mortgage, I'm forced to have one because without one I'm either renting or I haven't got a place to live. We don't need money—money's just an invention, isn't it? You can't run out of something you invent. It doesn't come from anywhere, we've invented it. And you cannot run out of things you invent, you just make more of it. They fuck about with the exchange rate and they fuck about with the interest rate and they fuck about with all that kind of side of it. But they can just print more money and they frequently do.

What we think we need, I suspect, isn't what we actually need. I need to listen to music. I don't need the latest pair of trainers or the latest car or, you know, a tin of paint [laughs]. Don't need any of that. Music enriches my life. I get depressed if I don't listen to music in a day. It's been part of my life ever since I can remember—one of my earliest memories is going absolutely bananas to a Neil Sedaka vinyl at the age of two, running round like a lunatic. Even now as an adult, I'll hear pieces of music which shake me to my core in some respects. As a species we've made music since we discovered we could bang bits of wood and blow into shells, haven't we? We've made music since the dawn of time, so arguably, music and art and those more esoterical things are actually needs, because they connect us.

I think fundamentally, if we all took more time out of our day to consider what we actually need, we might be a better society for it. Feeling valued—when there's a purpose to your being that has a positive impact on others. Maybe what we all need is time to think. Maybe that's really what we need. And capitalism gives you no time, does it, because it tells you when you have to be in work, it tells you when you can eat your lunch, it tells you when you can go home, it tells your kids when they gotta be in school. If all that were gone, we'd wake up when the sun rose and we'd go to bed when the sun set. We might lie about in that field all day.

123.

We had three ladies of mixed abilities, mixed ideas, but the thought was, *We're going to make a quilt.* And we were going to involve as many other people as we could. The idea just grew and grew and grew. We'd meet in one person's house, and then the next time we'd meet in another person's house, and gradually we gathered together people and ideas and materials and the whole thing started to grow. That's how we began to become a group. What it looked like then was a jigsaw but with no lid to look at. We knew we were all gonna make something to do with the nature reserve, something to do with the animal life, or the plants, or the geology, or the local industry. And gradually people decided what they would like to make their part of the quilt about. They all made one patch, one square. Some people lived far away and never came at all. Some people didn't want to be part of that group, they wanted to be part of the project but didn't want to meet up. Other people supported us by giving us materials but not sewing. And because it was not my idea exactly but my baby, I really wanted this to work, so I had myself, my mother, my son, and my granddaughter involved—four generations of our family.

Laying it out at the beginning, it looked like a pile of squares that could have gone in any order. I didn't want everything to be black or dark, didn't want anything to be too wacky, everything was natural colours and the one that was really bright yellow stood out, and that was the one that caught your eye and dragged you away from the rest. I think we used thirty squares in the end. We only wanted to use twenty-four, but we ended up using thirty. So now I've got strips of squares instead of a pile, and we left them out and took photographs, and you look at things and see how they fit together. But we had to wait till the end, really, to find out exactly what we were gonna have to play with. It's that bringing together and joining together and swapping ideas, and then making it all match up. It looks its best when it's hanging on the wall. It is fabulous.

At the beginning [it] was a very organised patchwork quilt with a lot of geometric design and set colours, and what it ended up looking like was totally different. The more people that joined us the more the ideas changed. It started off as three friends that gathered a lot of strangers around us, and by the end it felt like a huge great family. From nowhere we gathered all these strangers and managed to mesh all of our ideas and ended up with the most beautiful community quilt. And I can't tell you how proud I am of that [laughs]. We had the material quilt in front of us, and then we had the feeling of being a family, and being connected. We're never going to lose that.

124

I think decisions are always a little bit easier if you can imagine the future of those outcomes. You can go, *Okay, if I make that decision, six months down the line, what's that gonna look like?* Even on a really small scale you can go, *Okay, what should I have for breakfast?* You can have cereal or you can have scrambled eggs. If you have scrambled eggs, you'll be done in about twenty-five minutes, but you will have to scrub the pan a bit more, probably do a little bit more washing up. But you can visualise the near-future consequences of that decision. You have to think about the future in order to get there. And that's the problem at the minute. The future is so completely unclear, completely unwritten.

Because we don't actually have a future to look at, you can't imagine yourself there and reflect back, cos the outcomes are so vague. Your decision to go to the pub could mean your city ends up in a lockdown for the next three months. And that's also a joint, community responsibility. But nobody's talking about it. So I'd like it to all go to pieces and for everyone to just admit, *Yeah, I was a massive twat, I made a bad call there.* And then we can all talk about it together, hopefully. Yeah, make it fall. Collapse in on itself and be completely re-jigged, re-booted and re-thought. For everyone to just go, *Okay, this didn't work, let's try again.* I'd like for people to make better decisions everywhere, and be sure about them, and then be more honest than they usually would be even if it's a dubious decision. Say so, you know?

I do think that we're at a bit of a point now where there's no going back, really, and all the decisions are leading to more and more estuaries of confusion and difficulty for everybody. And it's killing people, literally. The wrong people are making the decisions, and there needs to be some kind of upheaval. I don't know how I want that to happen, because the idea of revolution, war, things like that, that's not something that I want to picture in my near future. However, I'm kind of skipping through that bit, and I'm imagining a world where we all grow our own veg and give it to our neighbours, that kind of thing. And you know, I think as we're losing all the beautiful social stuff that happens—even handshakes, *Cheers*, that kind of thing, all of those social cues are being completely rewritten—I think they should be rewritten so that more people can form meaningful connections with other people. I will continue to hope to persuade other people to be advocates for community, and for person-centred contact, and care, and for those to be the pillars that will hold up whatever's to come. And I hope the cracks start to show, even more, even if that means the tumble of everything. For me, you know—I'm probably privileged to say this—but for me, it would be worth it.

125.

I'm gonna desperately try not to get upset. But I am. My
husband died last year. In November. And that was why I
wasn't sure whether to do this or not. Because no matter
what I talk about it will eventually get round to that. He had
a tumour five years ago and they said he was fine, they tested
and all the rest of it. Then last April, last March, he became
unwell and he had pains and they said, *Well, it could be
gallstones or it could be your liver*. And him and I just looked
at each other and went, *It's the liver*, because that's where the
tumour would metastasise to. We got it confirmed in April.
And then from April it was the four of us, you know—the
boys were really good and they were very supportive. And I
think that brought them much closer.

They weren't particularly close when they were kids. And
it was something that R__ and I used to fret about—thinking,
Oh god, they're not going to be friends. R__, particularly,
because he had an older sister and a younger sister and he
always wanted a brother. So he found it particularly difficult,
you know, when the boys couldn't stand each other [laughs].

There's about three and a bit years between them, one's
thirty, one's twenty-seven. One's in London, one's here—
because of Covid and whatever he's been staying with me. So
he's had me getting upset and stuff like that. We're having a
conversation and then suddenly [I'm] crying for some reason
and he's thinking, *Oh shit—how did that happen?!* [laughs].
But they have stuck together. And I know that they talk to

each other a lot, and they come up with plans—because I was always the planner in the family. I was always the one that would say, *Right, we're doing this*, and then make it happen. But they've kind of taken that over. T__ will WhatsApp me at least once every day. He's the one in London. At least once every day, maybe some days two or three times. *How you doing, Mum? You alright?* You know. And J____'s the one [who] makes all the lovely food to keep me healthy. Because I'd just live on cheese on toast and pakora [laughs]. That's how I would get my vegetables, is through onion bhajis or pakora or something like that [laughs].

As a parent you sometimes, well, I know I did, I thought, *Oh god, I'm a really shit mum sometimes.* Like, *I'm really rubbish at this.* But I love being their mum as adults. They are good humans, good human beings. It's been them sticking together, I think. Cos one of the things was [that] their dad had made them promise that they would make me laugh.

No, no, I'm sorry. It's probably making it difficult for you. Oh, please don't feel bad. Cos, you know, it just happens. Like I said, I can be watching something on TV or listening to some music and I'm off.

126.

For me that's the whole point—to build your structure from the ground up. You're trying to construct an idea. Sometimes when you build up an idea, a concept, you're looking for the elements and you have to get those elements—all the pieces—together, and then you can start building. Blending all these different ideas and getting different analogies, and making connections, and making discoveries. The way you go about that, the ingredients you use, relates directly to what you produce in the end. You're trying to get the most elegant structure for whatever you're doing. So if it comes to designing product—because that's what I do—it's the way I link structure and assembly. They become one thing, really. I'm looking for a way to get these separate elements together. And in my case, they're manufactured parts, and I'm trying to get them to come together in a really elegant way, [so] that they almost self-support each other. Everything comes together in a moment on the production line.

But it's not just physical things. I'm also thinking about them as concepts that come together in that way as well. It's made up of so many different elements. It's a bit social, a bit technology, and you're also thinking about the people who are using it and you're thinking about the brand, and you're thinking about the suppliers. Those are all your structural elements, too. So you're building a structure, a piece at the end, that's made up of all these different parts that you're trying to fit together in an elegant way. You're thinking about relationships between people. You're thinking about materials. There's a lot of elements [and] you're trying to create this really elegant edifice at the end that kind of stands up by itself and doesn't fall over.

In scientific terms, it's that thing where you can't take anything away. You know, if you took something away the equation would fall apart. But I don't quite think of it in that way. I don't know what I mean by elegance really, except that you know it when you see it! There's that scientific, mathematical description of elegance but I think there's a cultural thing about it—you can look at it and say, *That's put together well.* You know, *I can see how all the elements come together.* It's not overdone. It's not laboured. It's just enough. And I think for me it's that elegance—knowing when to stop. Knowing when something is appropriate. I remember Elgar saying about Mozart that he reached the second simplicity. That's quite a nice thing. It's when you've kind of gone through the messiness and you've just got the little nugget that was there all the time. And a lot of other stuff has been stripped away. The complex meaning is still there but you've edited out a lot of the unnecessary. You might not understand the technicalities but you can sort of understand when someone else in another area has reached that moment of cleanness or simplicity.

127.

When I was a child, I had a phobia of frogs. Ranidaphobia, that's what it's called. I don't quite know what triggered it. I remember an incident where my brother and I were mucking about, he was fishing, and he pulled the rod back with a fish and the fish caught in my sandal. The fish was flapping at my feet, and I think that was the start of me being afraid of things flapping and jumping around my feet, but I don't really know what the origin of it was. Every time you run away from something that you're afraid of, it gets worse, it makes it bigger. So it went from me having this experience with the fish on the riverbank to not being able to walk in fields, because I was afraid that something was going to jump out at me. And frogs seemed to be everywhere. It was really weird, it seemed to know where I was. Whereas some people go, *I haven't seen a frog for fifteen years*, I was like, *I saw one yesterday! And the day before! They're everywhere!* I lived in a little cottage for a while when my kids were very small and it [had] a tiny little garden, which I was really pleased to have, and there were hundreds of bloody frogs in this garden. It was like, *I can't even go outside.* So that was one of the triggers. Well, it was that and also going to my daughter's nursery and not being able to go into the nursery to drop her off because there were tadpoles in the tank by the door. I thought, *I've got to tackle this*, cos apparently you can actually pass phobias on. If a child sees you being afraid then they'll copy you.

I ended up having some therapy/treatment to cure my phobia. I found out you're not actually scared of the spider or the frog or the scary lady in the picture or whatever— you're afraid of dying of fear. You're gonna die of fright. What they taught me was that when you're in a fear state your neurons are firing off, but after a while you can't be any more frightened and you will automatically calm down. It's like when you're laughing hysterically or you're crying cos you're really upset about something—eventually it stops because you can't do it anymore. It's the same with fear. What they taught me to do was to hold the moment and be in the moment, as opposed to running away. It involved me being in a room with a frog. It was hilarious, because I ended up standing on a chair, screaming. Then a cleaner walked in, and it was really embarrassing. She took one look at me and said, *I'll come back.* They call it 'flooding', what I did, which is you face your demon. They don't tend to do that as much now, for whatever reason. Maybe too many people stood on chairs and screamed while cleaners walked in.

128.

I just thought it was cheating [laughs]. Cos I was into drawing and painting and all the rest of it. And it wasn't till I got to New York, where I lived and worked for a couple of years, that I attempted collage for the first time. I didn't do it as a straight collage, I mixed a little bit in with my painting. Even if I'd worked twenty-four hours I couldn't finish the deadline with the way I painted at the time, which was very fine. So I thought, *I'm gonna cheat!* [laughs]. *I'm gonna stick a bit on here!* And I really, really liked the effect. I really liked [hesitates] the time, the time that came into it. Time in the sense of this historical bit of paper. Or the sort of three-dimensional aspect of it. All sorts of things. So I thought, *Ooh, I'll have another go at that.* It started to develop from there, really. It was a fluke in that sense. I mean, I just had this idea that it was cheating. It isn't, obviously, but for me personally, I thought it was lazy, a shortcut. Who knows, if the deadline had been longer, I wouldn't have done that and would've continued painting. But through necessity I found something that I really love and appreciate now.

The thing I like about collage is letting the accidents occur. You can't make mistakes on a screen. And if you do, you think it's a mistake so you try and correct it. No, you make the mistakes, you let things fall. Sometimes you've been working all day and you can't get it right and you look down on the ground and you think, *Oh shit, look at the way that's fallen. Pick it up carefully, bring it up here* [laughs].

That's what's so wonderful about it. I don't do collage work on computers. You think you're free but you're not. It's the restriction that makes you free. It's a bit like being locked up. How you going to get out? You're restricted, you gotta think outside the box and get out of here. What's around? Somebody has the bright idea of knotting old sheets together. Classic, old-fashioned way of climbing down out of a window. But you haven't got any sheets, there are no sheets on the bed. What else is there around? You have to look and you think, *Bed's made of springs, made of wire, maybe I can link them all together.* You would never think of it unless you were confronted with that restriction. And it's no different to creativity, really, because people just go with something they feel comfortable with. I don't really wanna be that comfortable—I wanna get myself on an edge where I think, *Woah, boy! What's going on here?!*

129.

We're humans, we seek patterns. That's part of what we do.

From when I was small, I liked making patterns with things. A toy that I loved very much when I was very, very tiny was some of these little tiles—which lots of kids have—you know, there's some triangles and some squares and different colours. And you could sort of make up mosaic patterns with them. And I really loved doing that. And then later on, I liked playing patterns with numbers and counting in different ways and seeing how the patterns would be and if you can make deductions. Again, this is a very small child thing, but I know it was before I started at school, because I was walking across the rec with my mum to collect big sister from [there]. And I was telling her very excitedly that I'd discovered that six times fifty is three hundred. And she said, *Oh, well done, dear, how did you [work that out]?* And I said, *It's cos it's like six times five but six times fifty. It's the same!* She went, *Yes. I mean, grown-ups do know that.* I was disappointed cos I thought I'd discovered it. She's like, *Most grown-ups would know that. But well done!* It was the six times five, six times fifty-ness of it. It was like, *This is it.* And it could go on. It's a trivial thing but it was interesting to me that it was a pattern that could continue.

And I think when it becomes even more amazing for me— it emerged that you could *prove* things. You can prove that there are infinitely many prime numbers. Like cast iron, this is true. It's been known for over two thousand years. That proof is still valid. It's not like science. Maths is the opposite of science, really. Was it Popper who said science is what you can disprove? It's testable theories. That's why religion isn't science, because you can't disprove God. It's a different thing. So science is something that is, in theory, disprovable. But you can prove things in mathematics. You can have mathematical proofs and if they're correct, you're done. So we don't still have the ancient Greek four elements—we have different science now and that's fine. But we still have those [mathematical] things that were proved, which is astonishing. And for me, it's one of the reasons maths is more like art. We can still admire ancient Greek art and it's still a wonderful thing. You know, we like modern things, too, but we can appreciate and admire art that was made a long time ago. There's an eternal aspect to it, which maths has as well.

130

I started collecting pineapple ephemera about thirty years
ago. It was a pineapple Britvic ice bucket that nailed it. I went
to boarding school and I used to go and stay with a friend
at her parents' place. It was a very lovely house, they had
beautiful antiques, it was a very old house. And then you
went into the kitchen and it was suddenly very modern,
and they had this plastic pineapple ice bucket. This was back
in the early seventies. And I remember thinking—a rather
snobby little twit, I was—thinking how very *vulgar* this
thing was, in this very elegant house with its Persian carpets
and lovely things. This naff pineapple ice bucket. But years
and years later, I went to visit a friend, and she had one on a
window sill, and I was like, *Oh! My god. I remember that!*
Actually it is a rather fabulous thing. And they said, *Well,*
you must have it. So I took it away with me, and then some
time later I was down in Bristol, I went into a shop, and
there was a pineapple light. So I bought that. And I have, I've
got an enormous, a really huge collection—hundreds and
hundreds of pieces of pineapple ephemera.

Kitsch is such a glorious thing, isn't it? I like the kind of
over-the-top-ness of the whole pineapple thing. But they
can be also extremely tasteful. They don't always have to be
brash, there are some very elegant things, and I have some
very nice pieces of pineapple jewellery. I have a beautiful huge
piece of Mexican folk art, which I had shipped back from the
States. And actually, as a gardener, in the horticultural world

there are plants that aren't pineapples themselves but look very much like a pineapple and I'm looking at one at the moment in the garden. It's a bulb called the *Eucomis*. It's a really beautiful flower with a spiky top to it.

Truth be told, we all have a collection in the waiting, because one of something doesn't mean anything, does it? Maybe you have two, maybe you have three, then you're off. I don't really ever have to buy them anymore because my friends go travelling and they see something, and over the years the collection has just grown and grown and grown. But more than anything, it really touches me, because people come back from travels around the world and say, *I saw this and thought of you*. There are these tentacles now, there are these threads amongst us all, there is this connection, as ridiculous as it is.

131

I finally managed to extricate myself from the sleeping, dreaming, waking limbo. I was lying there for I don't know how long. My hands were above my head, crossed at the wrists, and my legs were stretched out. It was almost as if I was tied by the dreams or they were trying to keep me in their grip. It's like there's a Plimsoll line—above the water is being awake, where I know I've got things to do. I know I need to record this. I know I need to get up because my boy is coming around to do homeschooling. Below the line is sleeping and the weird, disturbing dreams. And they're lining up. Strangely, at this stage, they're lining up like they're daring me to pick one of them to go down their bizarre little wormhole. As I'm in the middle of it, these weird images flash by, some cartoonish, others random—unfamiliar faces like adverts seen from a speeding train. As I say, it's taken me ages to drag myself out of this hypnagogy or hypnopompy. I'm not sure which it is. Apparently one is when you're trying to fall asleep, the other is when you're waking up. I'm not sure whether I was trying to get back to sleep or get up and do something, but I felt trapped in the middle.

The dreams are weird and disturbing. I don't know if it's a by-product of being locked down or my mental health problems or anything else. Sometimes it's very prosaic stuff that takes on a sinister, disturbing aspect. I was living in a shared house, renting a room in a house, I think. The people I lived with were at times familiar, at times complete strangers.

There was a very sinister atmosphere. At times, the kids were there with me and I must have been my age. Other times, I'm perhaps nineteen, twenty, and living in a shared house like I did back in the old days. I've forgotten a lot of the details now, like I always do. And I wanted to be able to give you more detail. All I know is that things like this leave me feeling really off-kilter for a big part of the day, if not the whole day, and I really need to drag myself out of it. It's very strange. I will try and get you some more at some point. At the moment this is all I've got. I've only just managed to open my eyes. I'm looking around at the room [laughs]—I know I'm awake now. Eurgh.

132.

I went out to Holland—we had a promotional cup which had a little tear-off thing on it and you could win prizes, and I needed this sorting. I was in mid-conversation with one of the Dutch guys about this promotion. Probably I was five minutes away from finishing. And he went, *Excuse me.* I went, *Sorry?* He went, *Five o'clock. I'm going.* What's going on? What's going on? Where's he going?! He went, *I finish at five. Nobody pays me after five. I start at nine, I finish at five. I do nothing before or after.* And that wasn't just him. They all went! They all went.

At the time, if I'm absolutely honest, I thought they were not particularly conscientious about the business that paid them their wage. And that's changed. Over the years I've thought, *Do you know what, they absolutely had it perfect. They're right.* Why would you work for nothing? Why would you work so many hours that you become effectively non-productive—or less productive? If you give a person ten units of work to do and they can do ten units of work, and they can do it well, you'll get ten good hours of work out of them. If you give them twelve units of work, not only will they not do ten, they'll probably be lucky to do eight. And the eight that they do will not be as good as the ten that they previously used to do. You overload people and you end up putting them under stress, you end up making them chase their tail, because they're trying to cover their tracks, they're trying to pick up on mistakes, they've lost their timetable, and they end up delivering a poorer performance. So it is a false economy.

Don't fall foul of living to work. You work to live. Don't live to work. It's advice that I don't think I've particularly taken on board for most of my life. Age is an enlightener. People have different perceptions of what old is, but for me, when you start to get round about mid-fifties onwards, you start thinking about your mortality a little bit more. It's then that you look back and you think to yourself, *God blimey, I made so many sacrifices for a career that actually didn't deliver any tangible benefit*. And don't get me wrong—I'm not trying to suggest that it's all woe, doom and gloom and everything else. However, however—whoever lies on their deathbed saying, *God, I wish I'd spent more time at the office*?

133

There's all sorts of cheesy aphorisms about doing things—
you know, *Feel the fear and do it anyway*, or whatever,
all those things. It's not very helpful, cos you don't know
whether it was useful until afterwards, so you can make
mistakes and you can have regrets. I really hate that whole
idea of no regrets. How can you not regret things? How
would you ever learn anything if you didn't regret stuff? It
can make you feel more of a failure. I don't have that kind of
simplicity available to me. I don't even know how to think in
that way.

It's feeling a little bit scary at the moment. I'm
unemployed and I'm trying to move into a new field, and
I'm older and I've just done some studies and, you know, just
feeling like I did when I was twenty-four or whatever. I'm
like, *Oh my god, I'm here again*, except I'm forty-three this
time. It feels like people aren't gonna give me the benefit
of the doubt so I'm quite afraid of what's gonna happen
to me, career-wise. I was trying to be a musician for years,
so I always had part-time jobs, quite nice ones. I ended up
having really nice ones towards the end. Then I got made
redundant. There's lots of reasons I didn't do that well as a
musician, and I can simply just say that I wasn't quite good
enough. Which is fair enough, but there's lots of people who
aren't that amazing who still manage to do something. I
think I was afraid of fully committing, of really going hard
for it, and I think that's what I'm trying not to do now. Not

compromise too much, because there's no point. You might as well go for it.

There's this Frank Ocean tune that I've been listening to a lot, and there's quite a cheesy bit, I don't know if it's his mum or an aunty giving him a bit of a lecture about being himself. I've never really understood what that meant, *Be yourself.* I'm like, *Pfft, who knows what I am? What you on about? What is that?* But it's been going round and round in my head. Sometimes those cheesy phrases make sense. I've started to think that is the key to not being afraid, in some contexts—accept that this is the kind of person you are and that's what you're gonna have to try and be.

134.

This took place some time in the mid-to-late eighties, with my family in _____, over Christmas. My brother was there without his partner/wife—don't know which she was at that point. Because before they had kids, he came to us and she went to her family. Made sense. My grandfather was there, who was quite a distinguished, important man, but also a bit of a shit. As my father used to say, or still says, *He didn't believe in family.* Anyway, he was sitting there in the first-floor drawing room of this beautiful house in the golden yellow armchair. I was in there with him, just him and me. And he said, in a rather annoyed [voice], *I didn't realise ____ wasn't coming for Christmas. I've bought her a present.* Rather than saying, *Why don't you give it to [my brother] and he can take it to her when he leaves?* I said, *I'll have it.*

So he handed it over, and it was something I coveted, cos there were a couple of others in the family. It was this beautiful wooden chopping board made by a proper craftsperson. My grandfather was very into crafts, particularly the potters but also the wood people. It's quite a thick board. I don't know what wood it's made from but between the slats that make up the board there's a beautiful inlay of a blue strip of wood and it was a very fine object. So I took it. I took it home [laughs]. And it's still there in my kitchen.

It's not what it was. It's very battered up, the little blue inlays are very faded, it's blackened at one end. It suffers pretty much every night from the massive brown slugs that somehow crawl into our kitchen in the early hours of the morning. And they just go for the wooden boards, so when you come down in the morning they're covered in slug trails. My brother and his wife _____ had three children. But when the youngest was ten, _____ died of breast cancer. That was nearly twenty years ago. And so every time I use this board, which is pretty much on a daily basis, I think of _____ . And it's good to think of _____ , but I think of _____ with a massive wallop of, *What a shitty thing to do.* And I hope that I'm not that person anymore.

135.

I am afraid of getting old, I'm afraid of dying, I'm afraid of getting an illness and dying, I'm afraid of getting a diagnosis [laughs]. I'm afraid of how I would react if I got a diagnosis. Would I be brave and deal with it? Would I suddenly really appreciate my life as it is and each day as it is? Or would I just hate everybody? And then how would I approach death? Would I like to find a nice rabbi?

I'm paying for my funeral costs [laughs]. I have this plan. My mum said to me, before she got Alzheimer's, she said to me, *I'll pay for the funeral.* And I just thought, it's really wrong that your mother should start paying for your funeral. There's something just not right about that. So I did, because I didn't know where I wanted to be buried and I thought I'd want the Jewish burial. I've been paying into this funeral plan that costs quite a significant amount of money but I don't go to the synagogue. Cos I don't really want to go there. But if I leave the synagogue, then I don't have the funeral plan because you can't take that package and apply it to a Reform synagogue, where I'd probably much rather be. Maybe it's like gym membership? You pay for gym membership and you don't go, you think, *Okay, I didn't do it,* then start with something else.

I feel that I've got to a point in my life where it's towards the end [laughs]. Kids moving out, everybody's parents are either dead or dying or old. I suppose the thing with Alzheimer's is that it's such a visible process of decay. And that whole thing of turning back into a child again, like a baby. That kind of helplessness. Loss, I suppose. I think maybe loss. Maybe it's loss. Loss of opportunity, loss of fulfilment, of being somebody or leaving a mark or a trace or something. How important is that? I guess it must be important because I'm talking about it. And then I think, *What's next?* In between what's next and death is the thing I'm at. This thing where suddenly years seem short. What am I going to be like as an older person? I don't know. I don't know.

I don't know.

136.

I believe in total predictability in the way things manifest, at least in my life, in the sense that some occurrences and re-occurrences seem to have a pattern. I don't really understand if it's me trying to find a narrative or if the pattern actually exists. Or if it's just me trying to pick out certain elements that might have a correlation with each other. That would be my answer at the moment.

As soon as I graduated from secondary school, well, before graduating from secondary school, about three months before, from one day to the next, my life came crashing—in the sense that I could not fathom anything anymore. Words had emptied out. I've never understood the clinical word for it, but I think it was like dissociations and psychotic beliefs or something, whereby I could not fathom certain concepts. It was very strange but I don't think it's incidental that these doubts aggressively came into my mind. They were entering my mind so violently. I could not stop them. I remember at some point I was not even going to the toilet because I thought that if I was going to the toilet it was not me going to the toilet but only a physical figment of me. It was very confusing.

But then, when I studied my degree, I learned that all these things that were bothering me and were stopping me from living life in the ordinary world have actually served as a basis for anthropology and cultural studies. The things we were studying could be used as a framework to analyse the crisis. I was able to recognise them by reading them. I understood that it is this *unknown* that is being studied, is being speculated on. I realised that it's not like I'm disconnected from the world—actually it kind of proves that I *am* connected to the world and that I perceive all the forces that draw me into the world. Although I didn't feel alive at that point, I realised that was the confirmation that I was alive. I try to use different perceptions and put them all into one flux. Like a stream, a flux in a philosophical sense, something that is going forward despite all of the contingencies.

137.

It's okay, but in the moment now, England, everything's crap. Because everything change. No work. So we can't sort it, our life. We struggle in the life. Everything is crap. Like myself, I lost my job, yeah? I've been in the company twelve years? And after that they've found out in my body I have a problem for operation. I been in operation for valve replacement so I can't sort it, my life, myself. So I'm happy about this, but the problem is we are not working. We are struggling. We're struggling for the life. Everything's no good. In the moment just we try to find some work. Very, very hard now. Very, very hard. Is no job. Just if you see something, you see the board say they look for the people, when you going there is no work. So we don't know what's going on now in England. Before it's not like this. Very, very difficult.

You know, I have two brothers and one sisters. We are here in the UK. All of them, they are struggling as well, the same problem. No work. Only one is working now. The one in Glasgow. For London is no working as well. But everything now in England it change, so we don't know the next generation what they are do. We pray God we can save this country as well. England's like our country. We pray God this country everything be fine. Give more work, more good people, good people in the Parliament, you know? And make people happy and the next generation they'll be happy as well.

My wife here sometime when we're walking on the streets, we see some people and they try to ask maybe some penny to buy some drink, you know? If she have it she give. Because we don't know. We don't know. Because the world is too short. Everybody in this world, we are like the [speaks French] *passagers*, you know. We *passagers*. We're going, we just don't know the place we stop. Like today it's me, I can drop in there or die. Everybody in the world like that. If you see something you need to try to help. Because you never know tomorrow.

138.

For the last two years I've had cancer and I've still got it.
I've got Hodgkinson's. I got the all-clear in January, that's
why we went on holiday, cos they said they've found more
now and I've got treatment from next week. That place there
is where they do all the electrical, electronic—not chemo,
when you have chemo you go to hospital—but there you
can have radio treatment. That's where I went first of all, I
spent three months in there having radio treatment. Which is
amazing—I thought it would be done in hospital, but it isn't,
it's done in an office block in the middle of town.

It's been hectic. I started off with bowel cancer and then
we got Hodgkinson's, but to the end. But I'm sixty-odd. You
expect things to go wrong. I've had a good life. I'm back on
the chemo next week. I had twelve sessions before I went on
holiday. You lose your hair, obviously, but it's growing back a
bit. You have your chemo, you go home, you feel sick, you're
tired, you're not well. Next day you're okay. And you've
normally got two week, two or three week, before your next
session. And you just live a normal life, you're just on tablets.

I think you make your own luck. I think if you're sitting
on the bench waiting for the lottery to come in every week,
that's not gonna happen. But you can make your own luck.
You can go and work hard, earn money and you can have
your holidays, have your flash car or whatever you want.
You know what I mean? As for fate, I don't know where
that stands. I think, wrong place wrong time, most of it,

313

isn't it? If something happens, it's like the wall falling on you—one minute earlier I hadn't've been there. I go through life thinking I owe nobody nothing, nobody owes me nothing, I pay for everything I get, and that's how I look at it. Nah, I don't believe in luck, not at all. I think you make your own luck.

139

This is gonna sound really wacky [laughs], but it feels like
our entire universe and us as beings is an act of creation.
And that ongoing, unfolding act of creation has a—is
purpose the right word? There's a teleology, that's probably
a better phrase. There's something teleological about the
way the universe unfolds and the way that we unfold and
our role within all of that. I've been fortunate enough to
have experienced altered states—if that's the right word—of
compassion and presence with another, and [with] nature.
It's not just brain chemicals and the wiring of the brain. It's
almost like the brain's a TV set and the consciousness—or
whatever it is—is actually all around us. I get those moments
when I'm in nature—and that could just be in my backyard
planting my potatoes or tending to the flowers—or when I'm
writing music or listening to music or writing. I just get into
contact with something much greater than me.

There's a real richness to living in the minutiae of simply
eating a meal or looking at something, and it's enriched my
life. Just by being, I think. And it's moved me politically to
a much more conscious position, environmentally. And also
it's made me a bit more relaxed about stuff [laughs]. I don't
know whether that's just getting older? Probably it's a bit of
both. That's actually a good example. I'm turning fifty in a
few weeks and I'm actually enjoying getting older. I've put
weight on and all that kinda stuff, and I can't do the things
that I used to when I was younger, but actually I'm enjoying

[it], and I think maybe that's part of it as well. Am I enjoying life more? Cos it's really fucking hard, actually [laughs]. So am I enjoying it more? Yes, yeah, I think so, yeah. Yeah. That's probably true. I think I'm enjoying it a bit more because I'm a bit more at peace with what happens, if that makes sense. Cos it's still really fucking hard [laughs].

140.

It was a really trouble. A really trouble for her, accommodation to the new situation. When she coming for example to first day at school. We don't learn English a lot in Poland. We are first communists as you should be know so, just like myself—I learn only Russian. That's it. And exactly when I come in UK I still try learning English every day with some books etcetera. Most of the time we spend in college. The college really helped for us. But for my daughter it's really hard for her going here when she can't speak to all the children in her school. And for now she really is great speaking English. She got a great job like me—more money like me, so that is fine. I'm really happy. She's for now really independent girl so I'm really proud from her and really happy.

We got a boy as well. For now he's ten. He's born here in UK. We're still trying saying the Polish language to him. For me it's important that he don't lost that Polish as well. We trying going for some holiday, spend some time with family, so normally when he come to Poland he speak in Polish as well. The Polish for him is a second language and sometimes he's like me in English and he is in Polish lost a lot of words [laughs]. So I try explain to him. For him for now English is first of all.

For myself, I start thinking—everybody is there. My brother, my sister, still in Poland. Father. Once a year, coming for only two weeks, it's a very short time, a really short time. Stress. When you see my hair, white, I think it's from stress.

But is normal. It is not my country. I try accommodate to myself and try accommodate to my family but it's still stress. We spend ten years here and sometimes I receive still stress. Stress with communication for example, yeah?

141.

I don't believe in God. I think it's ridiculous that in this day
and age people think that—I hope I'm not offending you—
that there's a superior being and that someone out there is
looking after us. I just think it's illogical, really. And that
makes me think I shouldn't believe in ghosts. But you see
some of those programmes and you just think, *Wow. That's
really, really something unexplained.* You know, you see
people do those ghost weekends and stay in a haunted house?
Absolutely wouldn't want to do that. That would scare me. I
think all that paranormal, supernatural stuff would be quite,
quite scary to me. And I have, sort of. When I was about
eighteen I worked in a pub. They used to talk about a ghost
in the cellar. We used to have to go down, change the beer
barrel, when the lager or whatever ran out. And one day,
someone sort of grabs me, or something grabs me, on my
shoulders. I leapt up. And there was nothing down there.
Everyone was up in the pub. There was no one around me. It
was so scary. So I've always had that in mind.

Is it a case that as you get older, you begin to understand
life better? So, you know, my fourteen-year-old is scared of
all sorts of illogical things and maybe as she gets older she'll
work that out for herself. That, you know, not everything
is scary. A lot of things aren't scary, really. I think my
conclusion is, rightly or wrongly, I'm not really scared of
anything. And anything I am scared of I have to just work
through. And you can explain everything these days, and

anything bad that's going to happen, I think people are resilient and will just get on and deal with. And those sort of situations where I would be fearful—staying in a haunted house—I just wouldn't put myself through.

142.

I remember it being in the afternoon, but it must've been in
the morning. I dropped my daughter at school. I'd got my
son with me, and I'd got him in the car and we must've been
one of the last cars in the car park. I reversed my car and I hit
another car, sort of sideways. The other car was facing ninety
degrees to where my car was facing. I really crunched into
it and really screwed up the side of the car. And I just drove
off. And no one saw. It didn't damage my car at all. It didn't
damage even the bumper of my car. And no one knows. Well,
you know now. And I know. And I sort of knew the person
whose car it was, but I didn't realise at the time.

It stayed with me for a long time. It's still with me now.
I feel really bad about it, when I think about it. It feels like
such a dark, strange set of feelings. At the time it hovered
around me for about three weeks—it kept coming back into
my head, made me feel really uncomfortable and guilty, I
suppose. Gradually, slowly, it faded—it was only a minor
incident, no one was injured. But still, it left me with such
a weird feeling. It made me think about people who get
away with more serious criminal acts and how you might
feel. And now there's something very disappointing about
dramas on TV, cos I don't think they ever get to the heart of
what it feels like to have done something wrong. To carry
that with you. When people commit acts of violence or
whatever, and then either do or don't get caught doing it.
Yeah, just don't really get to the heart of how strange and

unpleasant the feeling is that you carry around with you
having done something like that.

143

I was drinking a lot at the start of the year. The weather was good, you know, which is rare, the pubs were shut, and I was thinking, *Can't socialise, so I might as well sit in the garden and drink.* I was spending so much on beer. It wasn't sustainable. Then I moved on to gin and tonics [laughs]. You buy a bottle of gin for fifteen quid, and a load of slimline mixers, and that's only 115 calories, and it gets you shit-faced [laughs]. I felt unbelievably creative, those first few months. Potentially fuelled by drink, and also because [laughs], also because the kids were at home. I didn't have to keep going off to school, getting the kids, coming back, walking the dog, cleaning the house. Everyone was here. I did that, and then you kind of desensitise yourself to everything, don't you? It's a very numbing experience, although you feel very liberated, and you think you feel great. It was Father's Day, and I thought, *I have to see something different,* so we went to the beach early in the morning. A really good day—took the dog, kids running around, it was great, just like, *Ah, this is what I remember things being like.* Kind of like an electric buzz through your body. I just remember looking out to sea, being able to breathe, and I started thinking, *Okay, something has to change, I can't keep drinking like this. It's not doing anything for my health, not doing me any good physically or mentally.* I turned it all around and set up a little gym in the garage. At least I can come out of this—if we ever come out of this—feeling better, rather than just being drunk for a year. Very easy to do but very stupid.

144.

I was brought up as a Baptist. I did believe it for a long time. It was the only life that I'd known and I got really into it, in the sense of really studying it. And the more I got into it, the less I believed in it. But if I say I don't believe, that can't be proven either. I guess an atheist is somebody who definitely doesn't believe in God and an agnostic is someone who says, *I just don't know.* I was talking to my friend about this and we were saying it's really interesting how the idea of agnosticism—which is simply that you don't know—has become a very bad thing. In the age of social media everyone seems to have an opinion, and to have an opinion that's fully formed seems really important. Like, it's not okay anymore to say, *Actually, I'm agnostic, I don't really know.* On any subject matter. Everyone has to have a side, even though it's not entirely obvious to anybody—including politicians, I think—what the correct thing is. Everyone's got to have an opinion. You feel like you can't say, *D'you know what, I haven't studied the ins and outs.* Everyone seems to have an opinion fully formed and will violently defend that opinion. As soon as you've decided something, you've closed your mind. It doesn't give you any room to contemplate other people's arguments, to see where they're coming from. [Being agnostic] makes you more empathetic, perhaps? Maybe that's because of asking yourself questions like, *If I don't believe in God, then what's the point of being a good person?* I think it makes you question everything. It's the journey, not the decision.

145.

When I have sex with someone, I want to explore their body.
I really wanna go, *Okay, where are the spots on your body
that make you tingle in a way that maybe you never knew
before?* I wanna know everything about that person's body.
And I think that is literally like them accepting me for who
I am, for what my body is and what it does. And me doing
the same with them. That's crucial to having good sex. It's
something to do with touch that makes it easier as well.
When you're having sex with someone, you can kind of
tell by the way that they're touching you, whether they're
interested in you as a person, as a whole being, or whether
it's really just them trying to scratch an itch in some way.
Whether their heads aren't in it, whether their feelings
aren't in it. It's how they respond to you touching them, you
know, the way that they're touching you, if they are actually
paying attention to how your body is reacting to certain
things, if they listen to you whilst you're having sex. It's a
lot of different things. I've always seen it as something that
should be enjoyed by both the man and the woman—or the
woman and the woman or the man and the man. Basically by
all participants in sex it's something [laughs] that should be
enjoyed. I think sex is, in a way, like the ultimate yes. In that
you're giving your body to someone else and you're accepting
someone else's body into you. Yeah, the ultimate yes.

146.

My mother was a very strong, powerful woman. Still is.
But she was terrified of lightning. I have these very distinct
memories of being in a house in V_____, in front of a
big field lined with trees on either side. And as soon as the
thunder would start roaring in the distance, my mom would
immediately retreat to her room and go to bed, put the covers
over her, pillow over her head, and be asleep. And I would
be left to face the thunder and, you know, bolts of lightning
shooting down from the sky. In the menagerie of great
memories that I have there is that foreboding. And I think
it weighs a little extra heavy because it was just she and I. It
was just her and me, sorry [laughs]. My stepfather was not
fully in the picture at that point. So I dunno why, that just
sort of stuck as a secret recess that I don't really talk about.
And I guess it's more of a secret about my mother. But my
identity is totally fused with hers. And since we're in this
time of crisis, where we're sort of re-preparing ourselves for
inevitable departures, I think a lot about her being gone—
which she's thankfully not yet—but I think that memory
becomes extra pertinent. Because she would leave me and
I would have to face the world alone—in a very protected,
bourgeois way [laughs]. But still.

147.

The two of us were standing a bit awkwardly in a small,
barely furnished flat. It was about three in the morning.
There was a young woman sitting on her bed and she wanted
to die. We stood around and tried to let her have her own
thoughts—after all, she'd called us and let us into her flat.
We all needed to give it time. The woman seemed to be alert
and not as if she'd overdosed, so no strong coffee, no walking
her round the room. And then, after a long time, although it
was probably only about ten minutes, the woman said yes,
she would like us to take her to hospital. *I'll just pick up my
keys*, she said. And I suppose relief at getting an end result
went through us and our attention wandered, or slipped. It
was not keys but a razor she grabbed, and she slashed her
wrists so fast, it was too late to stop the cut as I took it from
her. She did indeed get to hospital—and live—but for a long
time afterwards I wondered what we might have said, or
failed to say, that would've brought the visit to a different
conclusion. There were other attempts on life, other moments
of someone's despair, they come and go, but this is one that
returns uninvited from time to time.

148.

I grew up by the sea, surrounded by sea. It's a very small
island, so it's something that I saw every day, interacted
with every day. I think what I like about it is it changes
all the time. One day it's flat, the next day it's dangerous.
Something about it just makes me feel better when I look
at it. Whether it is rough or still or whatever it is, when I'm
looking at it, it makes me feel better. I think it's because it
moves. The movement of it, the sound of it when it draws
the shells back or the stones back—depending what kind of
beach you're on. It's a bit like us. One day we can be flat and
then the next day we're raging. There's the horizon thing as
well. I love the cloudscape you get over the sea. You know,
when the clouds roll in? I don't know if you've ever been to
Devon or Cornwall, places like that? You might be on the
beach and you can see the storm coming in from miles away.
And I have a lot of respect for it, a lot of awe for it. It's very
powerful. And as much as it can be beautiful swimming in it,
it's fucking dangerous as well. It can kill you.

149.

It's about 10,928 days until I am in my seventies [laughs], so I haven't got long. I'm thinking I really do need a soulmate, a partner, for company, companionship and protection. I was nearly homeless a while back and there were a couple of friends that put me up for a bit, but obviously, when you're in your late thirties, forties, a lot of your friends have really young families, so it just scared me and I thought, *Wow, okay, I really do need to stop being so independent.* I tried two online dating apps, which were really good. Had some good dates. I'm friends with a couple of the men that I went out with. But I keep putting it off. I've decided now I'm gonna be proactive about that particular subject. I think I've had quite a dysfunctional background, not because of my mother but because of my father, and that's been my problem with men. So I've tried to be with women, and that's fine too. So I'm bisexual. I'm a bit confused. I'm not sure whether I'm cut out for relationships. But I'm friendly with all my exes, I think, every single one of them, even the one that I had a legal battle with—I'm friendly with him and his wife!

150.

There's this really annoying quote which always comes up
in academic writing. I don't know whether it's like a quote
from a person or just a thing that people say, but it's that
we write language and language writes us. Which sounds
super-wanky, but I think it links, because we feel like we use
language only to express ourselves better and truer and more
authentically and that it's a tool. And we then get trapped in
these language boxes.

I think you probably need a bit of self-awareness to even
understand that you're not [self-aware]. It's a bit of a vicious
cycle, because you need to look back and be like, *I'm not
expressing myself in the way I would like to, this doesn't
feel true.* That requires a kind of self-consciousness and self-
awareness as well. To know that it's not what you meant. So
it's working in both ways. It's kind of stopping you but also
making you clock that you are being stopped. Which means
you kinda recognise that you've put a limit on yourself.

And sometimes I think it's easier to ask for sex than it is to
ask for intimacy.

151.

Before I don't know to knit. Now I can do hats, cap, headband. Every day! At home! Watch TV! You have to be relaxing, because you can get pain in your shoulder, your back. You have to be relaxed—watch your TV and knitting. It help me. It keep my mind going. It help me so much. I did hats. A scarf. Socks, I didn't finish—because it's hard, very hard. This one is the lady teach me to do. I lost contact with her. When I was in detention, the Chinese teach me to do a box of flower with only piece of paper. Me, I forgot this one. Only knitting now! I did jumper. Because I have a grandson. I did jumper when he was three months, six months. But now he's older. Three months, I did jumper, hats. If I take my time to sit and do, one day I can finish. One day, I can finish. Like with crochet, it's very easy. No, my grandson, they are in France. Can't visit. No. They used to come. They promise me they will come in summertime.

152.

I believe that education is the most powerful force for good in the world, and that's why I've dedicated my entire life to it and always will. I grew up in a relatively impoverished situation. We certainly didn't have much by way of an advantage. I was raised by a single female parent who couldn't work cos she had a profound disability. And as children, we were, by most standards, in a pretty dire set of circumstances. What transformed my life in the long run was education. I met people in the school system and in the college system and then eventually in the university system that transformed my life in so many ways. And that's why I say I believe in education as the most powerful force for good in the world, because when I look at all the challenges I see anywhere in the world, I've yet to see a problem where education isn't ultimately the only sustainable solution. And I believe educators are the most important people in the world.

153.

The rat man came and set bait because we kept seeing a rat
out the back, in our garden, swinging on our bird feeder.
He's a freelance pest control guy because the council
have stopped all pest control during lockdown. He's a lot
more serious than the council guys about killing rats, and
suggested he set some traps. I was a bit uneasy about it, and
my wife really didn't want traps in the garden with the kids
playing, and with next door neighbour's cat, and hedgehogs
and birds and so on. But I said to her, *Do you want rats?!*
And she agreed, best to get rid of the rats once and for all.
So the pest control man set two traps, and said they were
hidden, and said they posed no threat to any other animals.
This morning, as every morning, I was woken by birdsong.
And I went out to check [it] and there was a female blackbird
dead in the trap.

154.

I really like these moments when I'm with my two children
and everything feels like it's perfectly in balance between the
three of us. And it's usually when something very mundane
is happening, like making some food, or just all being in
the same room doing different things. But I really like that
harmony. There's something about triangles, isn't there? It's
all about me with the children. And, you know, when they
were tiny, as the primary carer there was a lot of time when
it was me with them—eating, playing, bathing—and it takes
me back to that. I don't literally sit there looking at them,
thinking, *Oh, this takes me back.* But the feeling is similar
to those moments. And of course there are lots of moments
when it was all going pear-shaped and nobody was having a
happy time, but there were lots of moments where it was all
perfectly balanced. And it's nice, y'know. It's just nice.

155.

You don't know if you're sleeping, you don't know if you're awake, you don't really know what's going on and you wake up really confused. You know when you're in a dream and you don't know if you're watching or if you're in it? You don't know who you are in the dream? Then there's the whole thing in dreams when you're in a random place with a random woman sitting in a random area, this whole mixture of different worlds. These snapshots of different things together is like a dream. It doesn't not make sense—the same way when you're in a dream it doesn't not make sense—but then if you look closely into it you kind of think, *Why is that there? Why is that there? And that there?* All of these bodies and all of their different perspectives—you see all of them in the picture. You're seeing a whole different world of people.

156.

There's a part of me that's slightly embarrassed by how much of a socialist I am. And I shouldn't be. My *tadcu*, my grandfather, died a couple of years ago. He was ninety-five when he died. He was a communist. His family were communists. His dad was one of the first communist councillors in the Rhondda. And they were all part of the miners' strike but blacklisted for [it]. He would be very annoyed with me for being in any way embarrassed about this! His dad used to run a dancing school as well, cos he was a strike leader in the 1920 strike and he was blacklisted for doing that, so he couldn't work anymore. So he ran a dancing school and he was a councillor. They used to call him the Tap-dancing Marxist because he tap-danced, and then when people had come round and looked he'd start reading them *Das Kapital*!

157.

The first thing is freedom as intention and lifestyle, and that's difficult, man. You know, to be free of your own selves that ain't working, as well as the systems that one is a part of. That's the freedom to give love, receive love, share love, share joy. No matter what happens on a day-to-day, there will be a dissatisfaction unless you know that's why you're living, why you wanna live. But then again, after certain things—certain friends didn't make it—you reach milestones in your life, after which it's like, *Yo, everything here's now extra.* The joy of thriving is now appealing as opposed to the art of surviving. And that in itself is a furnace, right there. You know, it's a minuscule joy. The minuscule joy that's part of this umbrella of greater love. And to do that you've gotta do some warrior shit [laughs].

158

For me personally, I'm forgetfulness/dementia. I've told my doctor. What they want me to do is keep a diary, and I keep a diary. You know: *Last week I went to the door, locked myself out, couldn't find the key, knocked [on] my neighbour's door—'Help help help!'—couldn't get in. Where was the key? In my pocket! And I searched my pocket four times, it wasn't there. But it was in my pocket.* So to me [laughs]— you have to laugh.

Cancer is curable. Dementia, it's not. And your whole life, your whole life history, your family, your children, your grandchildren, is gone. I love my grandkids. I cannot even dream that I would never remember who they are and what we've done. No, no. You might as well take me away, you know. Might as well shoot me.

159.

If you've got more money, potentially you can have better healthcare, maybe extend your life, but there's a finite amount of time that everyone has in this world. A hundred and ten years, at a guess, is probably the most anyone really gets. Which is a speck if you look at it from a wider time perspective. So you've got your personal time, your day-to-day time, and then your lifetime. And how insignificant that is in terms of the time that the planet Earth's been around, and then the time the universe has been around. It levels us all to really a very similar place. And I think I personally have a lot of anxiety about time. About being insignificant and knowing I'm insignificant. And how I deal with that.

160.

When I was at school in Belfast, we had an RE teacher called
B_____ O__, who was like a fusty old bachelor, I suppose. He
had this strange smell. It was a combination of stale tobacco
smoke and old tweed jacket that probably hadn't been dry-
cleaned in a long time. And a bit of B[ody] O[dour] as well.
The overall effect, the overall combination, was this really
distinctive smell that, if I closed my eyes and smelt it, I would
know that was B_____ O__. Even quite recently, sometimes
I'll be walking down the street and I'll get this whiff of a
smell and it smells exactly like B_____ O__. And it's the
only time I ever think of B_____ O__. It's a weird, Proustian
thing, I suppose.

161.

What I tend not to speak about is that long before he became ill, even when he was in good health and there was no immediate prospect of his becoming ill, I prayed—insofar as it's possible for a non-believer to pray—that it would be my father who went first and not my mother. Not because my love for him was any less, but just because the pain and incapacity that he would experience on her death would debilitate him far more than they would my mother if he were to die first. Which isn't a secret, or even exactly an intimacy, just a sentiment I'd probably be reluctant to put my name to.

162.

I'll finish it on a really happy note. I took you down there
so I'll bring you back up again. In the simplest form, I love
waking up in the morning and the sun's out. Especially
in the current environment. Y'know, what we're living in
at the moment, it makes a hell of a difference when the
sun's shining. I can go downstairs, open the patio doors, the
little'un can run amok, wreck all me garden [laughs]. In the
simplest possible terms, it's lovely to wake up with the sun
shining. I mean, the sun's coming out there now, so I feel a
little bit happier.

163.

Sometimes the cattle stand very close to the fence, and you can hear them. Is it called ruminating? You can hear them chewing—chewing the cud—and it's really bloody loud. I hadn't realised that they actually kind of vomit up or bring up the grass they've already eaten and then re-chew it. It's a sound that I don't think I've ever heard in my whole life, but it's amazing seeing animals that big just hanging out and doing a lot of chewing. *Ruminating*. It's to do with digesting—digesting ideas, digesting and reconstituting ideas.

164.

It was just so eerily quiet and we really didn't know what to do. So we thought, *We'll just carry on as normal.* Driving to work, there was hardly anybody around. There was trees that had fallen over. There was one road where the tree completely blocked the road so I remember I had to do a detour round. It's just so, so unreal. Really huge trees that had been there probably a hundred years or so, been blown over, basically. The roots upturned.

165.

Both a desire and a fear is a fear of being stuck and having sterility. This kind of sterility of nine-to-five job, meat and potatoes, pay the bills, have a couple of kids and retire. This fear of that trajectory has been with me for quite a while. Now I'm feeling more comfortable, not overly settled, but more comfortable, just relaxing. To be in one place doesn't mean sterility.

166.

I realised that I've always had in my mind that if all else
failed, I'd be able to go and live there. Cos it was a house
with lots of bedrooms and it was like a sort of security
thing for me. And now, with my uncle's death, whose son's
thinking about selling the house, that possibility has been
taken away from me.

167.

You don't need a whole idea—a half, a quarter, a sliver of an idea is such a tantalising, enjoyable thing to chew on that it becomes something you cherish. I find that's really helped. No doubt it's a form of escapism, even if it's something very real. I've been thinking about the word *solace* a lot, in relation to that.

168.

He's actually built it back up into almost quite close [to] reality, hasn't he? It's obviously distorted around this bit in the middle, which is interesting. I don't know why you'd do that, particularly in the middle of where his mother . . . Oh, she's lost her hat, hasn't she? There's a bit missing.

169.

The only dreams I tend to remember is when my teeth fall out. Ever had one of those? It's quite a vivid, real feeling. The feeling of teeth falling out in your mouth. They just fall out. It's a mouthful of bones.

170.

I like every second of life. Oh yeah, I love life. I pay any money on the world to just give me two seconds. Two seconds more, mate. Because the planet is beautiful.

171.

It opened up my eyes to who I am and what life is all about. Well, not necessarily what life is all about, but just how insignificant we are as human beings.

172.

The time is flying, you know? I feel young, but when I see my son then I say, *No, I'm old man now.* Time is running so quick. That's true.

173.

I felt like I was a kid forever and now it's gone. In my brain, I am a massive kid, but my body is fucked, pardon my French.

174.

Bless them, cos every human being is wonderful. But they're easily led in a lot of ways and then it shapes their own demise.

175.

I was exactly in the place but I didn't understand. By now it was getting dark. I didn't know where I was going.

176.

There's no end goal to this. Death is an end, but it's not *the end goal*.

177.

It didn't come out great but it tasted good. That's what's important.

178.

You were gone.
You froze.
I can't hear you.

179.

180.

I want to stay and stay and never go.

WITH SPECIAL THANKS TO:

Aaron, Abubakr, Adriana, Aleem, Alex, Ali, Alice, Alokavira,
Amani, Andy, Andy, Anna, Anna, Anne, Annie, Anonymous,
Anonymous, Anonymous, Anonymous, Anonymous,
Anonymous, Anonymous, Anonymous, Anonymous,
Anonymous, Anonymous, Anonymous, Arran, Asheq, Astrid,
Barry, Belinda, Ben, Ben, Benita, Brandon, Brian, Brian, Bud,
Callum, Camilla, Caron, Catherine, C.C., Ceri, Dani, Danny,
Dauud, Dave, Dave, Dave, David, David, David, Denise,
Dimmus, Diya, Dominik, Eleanor, Emilia, Emily, Eric, Esyllt,
Flora, Frankie, Froude, Gaika, Gee, Gemma, George, Georgie,
Gigi, Gill, Greta, Harriet, Harvey, Heather, Helen, Ibrahim,
Issy, Istvan, Jamie, Janice, Jany, Jason, Jen, Jennifer, John,
Julian, June, Karen, Kate, Kate, Kenny, Knut, Koffi, Lauren,
Lee, Leila, Leon, Leon, Lisa, Llinos, Louis, Lucia, Marcin,
Marcus, Mark, Martin, Mathilde, Matt, Matthew, Maya,
Megan, Megan, Mel, Melissa, Michal, Mike, Mike, Mikesh,
Miriam, Molly, Nanou, Nick, Nina, Norah, Octavia, Owen,
Pattiiih, Paul, Paul, Paul, Paula, Paula, Pete, Peter, Prue,
Rachel, Ren, Rhys, Robert, Rochelle, Rose, Roxanne, Sam,
Sam, Sandra, Sara, Sarah, Sarah, Sarah, Scott, Sean, Shabaka,
Shafi, Silvia, Simon, Siofra, Sobia, Stan, Ştefan, Steven,
Stuart, Sue, Susan, Theresa, Tony, Tyson, Val, Walaa, Wayne,
Will, William, Yavuz, Zaeb, Ziggy, Ziri, Zoë.

ACKNOWLEDGEMENTS

Particular thanks are due to Nina Hervé @ Rough Trade
Books, Octavia Stocker, Gabriele Guercio and Lucia Coco
@ Juxta Press, and Sean Preston @ Open Pen, both for
permission to use sections of the works I published with
them in this book, and for the early and enthusiastic adoption
of this project and their support throughout. The three works
(*Rafal's Saga*, *When Is The Present* and *Not Far From The
Junction* respectively) slot on to this book and expand it in
various directions. Support our small presses!

Two of the sections included are taken from the
anonymised transcripts of focus groups conducted as part of
the research for Berwald S, Roche M, Adelman S, Mukadam
N, Livingston G (2016), *Black African and Caribbean British
Communities' Perceptions of Memory Problems: "We Don't
Do Dementia."* PLoS ONE 11(4): e0151878. https://doi.
org/10.1371/journal.pone.0151878

A lot of people helped me to find interviewees, but in
particular I'd like to thank Rochelle Scholar, Tom Hunter,
Carl Gosling @ Social Gathering, Andrew Gallix @ 3:AM,
Janet Hoskin, Niamh Goggin, Pat McGinn, as well as Heike
Langbein, Francesca Valerio, Micol Carmignani and all
the members of Migrants Organise: power in organising,
dignity in justice! Thomas Midgley gave me considerable
transcription help at a time when the job seemed overwhelming. Interview assistance came from Theresa Adebiyi,
Marcus Abel, Sean Preston, Miriam Ashon, Jonah German

and Aleph Ross. Reassurance and coaching was provided by Saul Ashon. Dan Crowe, David Wallace and the ghost of Cornelius Cardew helped me figure out the shape, possibly by accident. Special thanks to Alexa von Hirschberg, who seemed to see the whole thing even before I did, to Hannah Knowles, Mo Hafeez, Kate Ward, Ian Critchley, Ian Bahrami, Jon Gray, Hannah Marshall, Josh Smith, Lizzie Bishop, Hayley Benoit, and everyone else at Faber & Faber and beyond who worked on the publication, distribution and sale of this book. To Patrick Walsh, John Ash, Margaret Halton and everyone @ PEW Literary. To the friends who gave up time and brainpower discussing it all with me, in some cases endlessly: Nick Midgley, Max Porter, Alastair Siddons, Matthew Shapland, Miriam Ashon, Will Atkins, Matt Thorne, Lesley Thorne, David Townsend-Elliot, Marcus Abel, Simon Skevington, Yuval Etgar and Lucy Kirkwood. Thanks and apologies to the people who gave up their time to talk to me and whose words, for a variety of reasons, I couldn't use in this book: Angus, Ana, Aren, Grace, Haifa, Ion, Jai, Jonah, Jonny, Jordan, Josh, Kirsty, Krzysztof, Lil, Mo, Paul, Stefan, Stuart, Stuart and Yuval.

Last of all, thanks to Leila Baker, for constant advice, support and encouragement throughout the whole process, including your work as my one-person, 24/7 ethics committee. You did more for this book than anything else I've written, which is probably why it has so much heart.